ENCOUNTERS WITH PAUL

A modern mosaic of the image of Paul and Thecla painted in the cave above the ancient site of Ephesus. The Acts of Paul and Thecla is a second century document about a female follower of Jesus, and disciple of Paul.

ENCOUNTERS with PAUL

by
*Ben Witherington III
and Ann Witherington*

CASCADE *Books* • Eugene, Oregon

ENCOUNTERS WITH PAUL

Copyright © 2024 Ben Witherington III and Ann Witherington. All rights reserved. Except for brief quotations in critical publications or reviews, no part of this book may be reproduced in any manner without prior written permission from the publisher. Write: Permissions, Wipf and Stock Publishers, 199 W. 8th Ave., Suite 3, Eugene, OR 97401.

Cascade Books
An Imprint of Wipf and Stock Publishers
199 W. 8th Ave., Suite 3
Eugene, OR 97401

www.wipfandstock.com

PAPERBACK ISBN: 978-1-6667-3452-2
HARDCOVER ISBN: 978-1-6667-9045-0
EBOOK ISBN: 978-1-6667-9046-7

Cataloguing-in-Publication data:

Names: Witherington III, Ben, and Ann Witherington.

Title: Encounters with Paul / Ben Witherington III and Ann Witherington.

Description: Eugene, OR: Cascade Books, 2024 | Includes bibliographical references.

Identifiers: ISBN 978-1-6667-3452-2 (paperback) | ISBN 978-1-6667-9045-0 (hardcover) | ISBN 978-1-6667-9046-7 (ebook)

Subjects: LCSH: Paul, the Apostle, Saint | Apostles—Biography | Bible stories—New Testament

Classification: BS2506 W55 2024 (print) | BS2506 (ebook)

Please note that ALL photographs in this book are pictures taken by the author, unless otherwise indicated.

CONTENTS

Introduction vii

The Dramatis Personae ix

In the Words of Gamaliel—Saul's Teacher 1

In the Words of Ananias of Damascus—Saul's Baptizer 5

In the Words of Barnabas—Paul's Companion 9

In the Words of John Mark—Paul's Off-and-On Friend 21

In the Words of Silas / Silvanus—Paul's Second Journey Companion 27

In the Words of Euodia—One of Paul's Many Converts 34

In the Words of Sergius Paulus 39

In the Words of Demetrius, The Silversmith—Paul's Nemesis in Ephesus 42

In the Words of Titus—Paul's "True Son" 46

In the Words of Crispus, The Synagogue Leader—Paul's Convert in Corinth 50

In the Words of Gallio—Paul's Judge in Corinth 53

In the Words of Apollos—Paul's Colleague in Ephesus and Corinth 56

In the Words of Priscilla—Paul's Most Famous Female Co-Worker 62

In the Words of Phoebe—Paul's Female Deacon 67

In the Words of Felix—Paul's Procurator and Jailer 73

In the Words of James, Brother of Jesus—The Christians' Spiritual Leader in Jerusalem 76

In the Words of Timothy—Paul's Best Friend 82

CONTENTS

In the Words of King Herod Agrippa II—Paul's Nemesis 86

In the Words of Julius the Centurion—Paul's Escort to Rome 91

In the Words of Eutychus—Paul's Fortunate Friend 96

In the Words of Junia—Paul's Friend and Apostle 99

In the Words of Nero—Paul's Executioner 104

In the Words of Luke—Paul's Physician and Scribe 107

In the Words of Simon Peter—Paul's Counterpart in Missions 112

In the Words of Clement—Paul's Successor in Rome 117

Epilogue 121

INTRODUCTION

IN 1990 MY WIFE, Ann, me, and our two children went on our Wild West tour. We flew to New Orleans and drove to San Antonio, Carlsbad Caverns, Tucson, the Grand Canyon, Grand Junction, Silverton, Aspen, and Denver. While driving through the desert in Arizona, we visited the largest meteor crater in the United States. This privately owned hole in the ground is about 3,900 feet wide and 560 feet deep, big enough to hold twenty football stadiums. It has rightly been said that you can judge the size and importance of something by the impact it leaves behind. There is nothing but bits of rock left from that meteor, which weighed about 150,000 tons before it landed!

The same can be said about the Apostle to the Gentiles—Paul. You can't find him anywhere today, but his impact is evident all over the world. Other than Jesus, no one made a bigger impact on the early Christian church than Paul. Similarly, other than Jesus, Paul was also the most controversial figure in early Christianity. Unlike Jesus, however, the Apostle to the Gentiles traveled far and wide in the western end of the Roman Empire, from Jerusalem to Rome across the northern lands bordering the Mediterranean. In all those travels he met hundreds if not thousands of people from about the mid-30s to the mid-60s AD. During that time, he persuaded many to become followers of Jesus. He also irritated and even enraged a lot of people by his proclamations of the good news and by his exhortations about the need for subsequent behavior changes! He was a human lightning rod, and very few people had the capacity to simply ignore him. They were either shocked and revolted by what he said and did or surprised and changed by his message and methods. And this was true not only when he visited synagogues in the empire, but also when he was talking to Gentiles in forums, homes, lecture halls, jails, and elsewhere. Later, he was even accused of being the inventor of Christianity, not to mention a great perverter of both early Judaism and the message of Jesus of Nazareth.

INTRODUCTION

Thus, this book is written from the perspective of those who knew Paul whether for a short or long time. They are allowed to tell their first-century stories to a twenty-first-century audience which, hopefully, will lead to new insights about this enigmatic man.

In earlier studies, particularly *The Paul Quest* (1998), commentaries on Paul's letters and Acts, and most recently *Voices and Views on Paul* (2020) written with Dr. Jason Myers, I have dealt at length with the voluminous discussion on Paul, which continues to cause controversy and debate. In fact, one could say there is an *appalling* amount of books and articles on Paul!

This little book is altogether different—a work of historical fiction or, better said, careful historical conjecture trying to fill in the gaps in Paul's story. It is intended as a companion volume to my *Encounters with Jesus* (2020). In this little study I think creatively about the various people we know from Scripture who encountered Paul and I let them share their impressions of this controversial man. It is enlightening to see Paul through the eyes of those who encountered him directly and personally, whether briefly or over a long period of time, including those who shared Paul's faith in Jesus the Christ and those who did not. Without question, Paul left an impression on them all. He was often misunderstood in the first century and still is today. Was he a paradigm of what it means to be a follower of Christ, or a pariah that misled people? Franz Overbeck once said about Marcion, a second-century heretic, that he was "the only Gentile Christian who understood Paul, and even he misunderstood him." Perhaps the following study will help us, especially those of us who are not Jews, understand the Apostle to the Gentiles a bit more.

From time to time, I have used the 1984 NIV edition to fill in the gaps, with permission of Stan Gundry at Zondervan Press. Occasionally I have altered this text when I thought the translation could be improved. I am grateful for the pictures in this volume from the websites of my colleagues Carl Rasmussen and Ferrell Jenkins. Thank you for letting me use them! Other pictures are either my photos or available in the public domain.

Ann's role in this book was to check the consistency of what was said, smooth out any rough spots, clarify if something seemed obscure, and at the same time if she thought something more was needed, she would do a bit of final research.

SUMMER 2023

THE DRAMATIS PERSONAE

1) GAMALIEL
2) ANANIAS
3) BARNABAS
4) JOHN MARK
5) SILAS
6) LYDIA
7) SERGIUS PAULUS
8) DEMETRIUS THE SILVERSMITH
9) TITUS
10) CRISPUS THE SYNAGOGUE LEADER
11) GALLIO
12) APOLLOS
13) PHOEBE
14) PRISCILLA
15) FELIX
16) JAMES, BROTHER OF JESUS
17) TIMOTHY
18) KING HEROD AGRIPPA
19) JULIUS THE CENTURION
20) EUTYCHUS
21) JUNIA
22) NERO

THE DRAMATIS PERSONAE

23) LOUKAS
24) PETROS
25) CLEMENT

IN THE WORDS OF GAMALIEL— SAUL'S TEACHER

Gamaliel the Elder was a well-respected Jewish religious leader in the early first century. Historians believe he was a Pharisee. As an expert in the Jewish Mosaic law, he was a member of the Great Sanhedrin, which met in the Jewish temple. In short, he was held in high esteem. And Paul himself is proud of the fact that Gamaliel was his teacher (Acts 22:3). As the fledgling church grew, Gamaliel wisely encouraged other Pharisees in the Sanhedrin to carefully evaluate all the apostles of Jesus (Acts 5:34–39). In his own words: "Therefore, in the present case I advise you: Leave these men alone! Let them go! For if their purpose or activity is of human origin, it will fail. But if it is from God, you will not be able to stop these men; you will only find yourselves fighting against God" (Acts 5:38–39). Let's hear from this wise man.

Rabban Gamaliel (רבןגמליאל) as depicted in the Sarajevo Haggadah, a 14th-century illuminated manuscript.

ENCOUNTERS WITH PAUL

Oh yes, I certainly remember Saul of Tarsus! He was truly unforgettable in numerous ways. I had never seen a disciple advance so rapidly in knowledge of Torah and our traditions. He was very bright, with a razor-sharp ability to get to the heart of matters quickly. And he had a memory like that old saying of Shammai, "To what shall we liken a good pupil? He is like a cistern not losing a single drop poured into him."

And then there was the young man's zeal. You have to realize he came to Jerusalem from Tarsus as a young man. He was brought here by his parents because they realized that in Tarsus there just weren't teachers who could answer his questions and guide his education.

When Saul arrived, Judaea was in turmoil. All of a sudden Herod Archelaus was no longer governing us—we had come under direct Roman rule with a Roman governor. Devout Jews, while they had not liked the Herods very much, liked the pagan Romans even less. The Romans seemed clueless about the traditions of the Jewish people and their belief in one God. There were lots of angry discussions and heated exchanges during this time between the Jewish and Roman leaders.

When Jesus of Nazareth was crucified by the Romans just outside Jerusalem's city walls, we thought some of the internal divisions amongst Jews might be healed. Abandon hope! The most ardent followers of this Jesus claimed shortly after his death that he had risen from the dead, appeared to them, and even commissioned them to proclaim this new messianic form of Judaism to both Jews and Gentiles! This was clearly too much for Saul!

Already zealous in regard to pagans ruling Judaea, the notion that even Jews were departing from their traditions and the strict teaching of Torah was too much for this volatile young man. He decided a campaign against "the Way" as it was called (as if there was only one way to do our faith properly) was imperative. He even went to the High Priest to get a commission to bring these so-called renegade Jews before the Sanhedrin for judgment for blaspheming Yahweh. Who had ever heard of a crucified and risen messiah? No one who had closely read the prophecies of Isaiah and others ever interpreted them that way.

And crucifixion—it was the most shameful way to die in our world. Some Jews even connected it with the saying from Deuteronomy 21:22–23, which claims "cursed be he who hangs upon a tree." They took that to mean Jesus of Nazareth, who got himself crucified, clearly must have been cursed, not blessed, by Yahweh. I myself would not have gone that far, but then Saul's zeal was more extreme than mine.

IN THE WORDS OF GAMALIEL—SAUL'S TEACHER

Unfortunately, the debacle of going to the Hellenist synagogue in Jerusalem and dragging off Stephen for stoning did not satisfy Saul's zeal. Instead of being satisfied that he had done his duty to his faith, he decided to go on a campaign to other places in Judaea, even as far as Damascus, to bring others to justice for blasphemy. I tried my best to warn Saul by saying that if this new movement is not of Yahweh, may he be blessed forever, then it will die out like other movements involving false messiahs. But if this movement is from Yahweh, then you will not be able to stop it! Indeed, you may even find yourself in opposition to his will!

But Saul had the bit between his teeth. He would not listen even to his old teacher. He went off to Damascus—and then something happened! I do not really know what happened. All I know for sure is that Saul's campaign came to a screeching halt! Then there were reports that he had done a complete about-face and become a follower of this Jesus of Nazareth. Incredible! How could someone change their convictions that drastically and suddenly? Perhaps his mind just snapped—I don't know. What I do know is, he'd better not show his face in Jerusalem any time soon. Not only will the Jewish authorities want to deal with him, but these new followers of "the Way" are scared to death of him because of Stephen's death.

I have wracked my brain trying to figure out if something I taught Saul had helped precipitate this tragedy. Could it have been our many hours spent examining the Isaiah scrolls, especially the parts about the suffering servant? Could it have been my advice to study rhetoric so he could more persuasively share our faith? Could it have been the fact that I had taught that there were many schools of thought in Judaism, whether one listened to Shammai or Hillel or others? Could he have come to think of "the Way" as just one more messianic way of practicing our faith? I do not know.

But perhaps I was right, since this messianic movement called "the Way" keeps spreading and gaining more adherents. Perhaps I was right that Yahweh had something to do with this, which I just don't understand. Isn't a crucified messiah a contradiction in terms? Isn't the true messiah supposed to be like David? Why didn't this Jesus reestablish the monarchy and defeat the foes of Judaism?

Most recently, the person that has surprised me most is Jacob the Just,[1] the very brother of this Jesus. He had not been a follower of his brother Jesus at all during his earthly ministry in Galilee and Judaea. To the contrary, he thought his brother misguided despite all the reports of healings and the

---

1. The actual name of Jesus' brother, whom we call James.

like. But I heard that Jacob claims he saw Jesus alive in the flesh after his crucifixion. As a result, Jacob apparently changed his whole way of evaluating his brother. Astonishing! What's next?

The prophecies can be interpreted in various ways. Perhaps it is just as well that Yahweh only reveals enough about the future to give us hope, but not so much that we don't have to live by faith every day. May the Lord bless us and keep us in this tumultuous time.

IN THE WORDS OF ANANIAS OF DAMASCUS— SAUL'S BAPTIZER

Ananias was a disciple of Jesus who conveniently lived in Damascus when Saul had his conversion experience. The story of Ananias in Acts 9 is full of surprises. Jesus himself (in a vision) told Ananias to go to the home of a man named Judas on "Straight Street," where he would find Saul of Tarsus. At this point, both men were probably afraid. Saul's persecution of the followers of Jesus was well known. And Saul himself had just been blinded on the road to Damascus! Eventually, Saul would tell his listeners that Ananias was a "devout man according to the law, having a good report of all the Jews that lived in Damascus" (Acts 22:12). Ananias of Damascus will have much to say about his amazing time with Saul of Tarsus!

The Baptism of St. Paul by Ananias;
12th-century mosaic,
the Palatine Chapel, Palermo, Sicily.

I was scared! In a vision I was told to help Saul of Tarsus, but he was the very man who was coming to Damascus to take followers of Jesus captive and haul them off to Jerusalem for trial! Could this be a trick or a trap? Could the man be pretending to need help or pretending to have changed his mind about Jesus? Had I really understood the vision clearly? If it was true that Saul had changed, he would be *persona non grata* with Jews who did not follow Jesus and suspect to those who did. Apparently, Saul had been abandoned in a house on Straight Street belonging to Judas, a man I knew by name only. I was afraid to go knock on his door, but equally afraid to be disobedient to the heavenly vision.

Truthfully, I tried to object to the heavenly voice and said, "Lord, I have heard many reports about this man and all the harm he has done to your holy people in Jerusalem. And he has come here with authority from the chief priests to arrest all who call on your name." But the Lord said to me, "Go! This man is my chosen instrument to proclaim my name to the Gentiles and their kings and to the people of Israel. I will show him how much he must suffer for my name."[1]

So, with much trepidation, I went and gently knocked on Judas's door. I was ushered in to a room where a bearded man was lying on a makeshift bed, praying fervently. My instructions were to lay hands on the man, as he needed healing and I could see that his eyes were caked shut by some kind of substance. I got out my bottle of olive oil and a small cloth and began to gentle wipe his eyes clean. He whispered, "Ananias, is that you?"

I cleared my voice and replied, "Brother Saul, the Lord Jesus, who appeared to you on the road as you were coming here, has sent me so that you may see again and be filled with the Holy Spirit." To my astonishment, something like scales fell from Saul's eyes and he could see again! He got up and asked for baptism. So, I baptized Saul with some water from the purification jar in the house. After this, Judas's wife persuaded Saul to take some food. After all, he had been fasting while praying. Quickly, he regained his strength. Though he could see again, I noticed that his sight was not completely perfect. He kept squinting and his eyes watered as was evident even in the lamplight.[2]

---

1. Here it seems likely that "Lord" means the Lord Jesus, just as it does in the vision Saul had on Damascus Road. Ananias was a Christian disciple who had learned to call Jesus the risen Lord.

2. Scholars have speculated as to what Paul's thorn in the flesh was, and what sort of malady he suffered from while in Galatia (cf. Gal 4:13–15 and 2 Cor 12:7–8). The Galatians text is revealing because it hints at ancient beliefs about the evil eye. Eyes were viewed as the windows on the inner person—as projectors rather than receptors of either light or darkness. If one thought someone was giving another "the evil eye," one response was to look away and to spit to ward off the potential evil influence. Paul says in Galatians 4 that instead of spitting and rejecting him, they treated him as an angel sent from God with the good news. He adds, "You would have plucked out your eyes and given them to me." This cannot be a random remark. In 2 Corinthians 12, Paul talks about an ongoing

IN THE WORDS OF ANANIAS OF DAMASCUS

I wanted to hear Saul's story, particularly the most recent part of what happened on the road to Damascus. As it turned out Saul was quite the storyteller. This is the essence of his tale as I remember it. Saul said to me:

"I am a Jew, born in Tarsus of Cilicia, but brought up in Jerusalem. I studied under Gamaliel and was thoroughly trained in the law of our ancestors. I was zealous and I persecuted the followers of "the Way" to their death, arresting both men and women and throwing them into prison as the high priest and all the Council can themselves testify. I even obtained letters from them to their associates in Damascus and went there to bring these people as prisoners to Jerusalem to be punished. About noon, as I came near Damascus, suddenly a bright light from heaven flashed around me. I fell to the ground and heard a voice say to me, 'Saul! Saul! Why do you persecute me?' 'Who are you, Lord?' I asked. 'I am Jesus of Nazareth, whom you are persecuting,' he replied. My companions saw the light, but they did not understand the voice of him who was speaking to me.

"'What shall I do, Lord?' I asked. 'Get up,' the Lord said, 'and go into Damascus. There you will be told all that you have been assigned to do.' My companions led me by the hand into Damascus, because the brilliance of the light had blinded me."

I asked Saul to say more about his vision. He said that while the vision was directed to him personally, those who were with him saw a light and heard a sound, but unlike him they did not see a person and hear a voice speaking words. It was Saul alone who was being confronted and given clear instruction, but his companions knew something extraordinary was happening.

---

painful condition ("a stake in the flesh sent from Satan") that was bothersome but not severe enough to prevent Paul from being a missionary. To this we need to add two things. First, why did Luke the physician travel with Paul on part of his second and all of his third missionary journeys? Could it be because Paul required treatment for a chronic condition? Second, why would Paul, a literate man, need scribes to write his letters? Note that Paul sometimes says that he is picking up the pen to sign the letter—"see with what large letters I write my name. This is the way I write in all my letters." This points to a person with eye problems. From Acts 9:22, 26 we know Saul was blinded to such a degree that he had to be led by hand into Damascus. We also know he received back at least partial sight. The Corinthians complained that while his letters were weighty his physical state was objectionable. He didn't look right and they didn't like the way he pronounced Greek either (2 Cor 10:10). And who can believe a seer who can't see well? Paul was tortured various times, which probably didn't help either!

The irony is, he didn't even know who was confronting him from heaven. He asked, "Who are you, sir?"[3] The voice from heaven had asked, "Saul, why are you persecuting me?" That seemed an odd question as well, but one which connected Jesus with his earthly followers, and at the same time made clear this was no mere angel talking to Saul. It was someone much greater.

The encounter had begun to change Saul's life forever. The one who had been inflicting suffering on Jesus and his followers was now going to suffer for Jesus and his followers. If Jesus was alive in heaven at the right hand of Yahweh, then Yahweh must have vindicated him beyond his horrible death. Saul, being a Pharisee, had no problems believing in the idea of the resurrection, but in fact none of us had anticipated a crucified and risen Messiah, much less one exalted to the right hand of Yahweh. And none had expected the resurrection of a single person, the Messiah, when God's final salvation began to come. There was much to process.

After a few days, Saul felt well enough to share his story in the local synagogue but it was not well received, and the end result was that Saul went off to Nabatea to Arabian Petra, to make a fresh start as a follower of Jesus. And he was there for some years.[4]

Always the subject of controversy, when Saul finally returned to Damascus, he had to leave quite quickly. The ethnarch of King Aretas of Nabatea was after him and had come to Damascus to take him into custody. We had to lower him in a basket over the city wall for him to escape the ethnarch! What a day that was![5]

We later heard he went to Jerusalem to meet particularly with Simon Peter. I do not know how that meeting went. What I do know is that wherever Saul went, controversy followed. By the way, he calls himself "Paul" now. I pray for his safety regularly and that he fulfills his commission from the Lord.

---

3. The word "kyrie" in the vocative is a term of respect, like the English word "sir." Saul was not addressing Jesus as the risen Lord.

4. This story is told in my book *Paul of Arabia* (2020).

5. 2 Cor 11:32–33.

IN THE WORDS OF BARNABAS—PAUL'S COMPANION

Barnabas was raised by his Jewish parents, both Levites, on the island of Kupros, Greek for Cyprus. As a child he was called Joseph. In Acts 4, he is living in Jerusalem, selling a field, and giving the money to the apostles for distribution to the poor. At this point Joseph is already being called Barnabas, and he rose to become a prominent disciple and missionary. Acts 14 refers to him as an apostle. Barnabas encouraged the new believers in Antioch (Acts 11), brought Paul to Antioch, mentored Mark when Paul refused to work with the lad (Acts 11), and traveled on Paul's first missionary journey (Acts 13). One of their biggest problems was the Judaizers who wanted Gentile converts to technically become Jews first (even to the point of being circumcised). To resolve this problem, both he and Paul attended the Council of Jerusalem around AD 49. Imagine the stories Barnabas could tell us.

Icon in St. Barnabas Monastery, Salamis, Cyprus. The monastery traces its origins to AD 475. The current edifice, built in the 1700s, is now a museum.

ENCOUNTERS WITH PAUL

It's good to be back on Kupros! That's Greek for the island of Cyprus in the Mediterranean, where I grew up. Life was good here far away from the chaos in Jerusalem and elsewhere. I have many memories of my first return here with Saul of Tarsus. We had been commissioned to be *apostoloi* from the community of Antioch to begin sharing the good news elsewhere in the Empire. I thought that my home region was a good starting place. I had no idea Saul intended to go elsewhere after we evangelized Cyprus but, as usual, Saul had surprising plans. For a younger man he seemed very sure of what needed to be done. The call of God on his life was evident. He was a man in a hurry to get on with that call and commission, and he wasn't going to let misfortune slow him down. His drive and energy were breathtaking. In fact, it makes me tired just thinking about all we did on that first missionary expedition. But perhaps it would be good if I backed up and told the story of how I met Saul in the first place.

My proper name is Joseph, and I descend from a Levitical family. As a Levite, I had gone to Jerusalem on various occasions to further my education. Early on when the Way was just beginning to be a force among Jews in Jerusalem, I came into contact with Simon, James, and others, and became a follower of Jesus. Almost immediately they gave me the nickname Barnabas, which could mean "son of a prophet" or "son of encouragement." In any case I became deeply involved in this new Jewish movement.

My family was relatively well off, and we owned property in Jerusalem. At one point I sold a field to replenish the resources of the Jerusalem community and gave the funds to Peter and John.[1] I was there on that horrible day Stephen was stoned. I saw Saul of Tarsus watching and approving. He seemed too zealous in enforcing our Mosaic law, and too quick to quell views he saw as blasphemous. I did not like the look of him. He had zeal but not according to the broader interpretation of Torah. The heart of the Law is mercy, something that became all the more evident to me when I became a follower of Jesus.

Some years later, Saul returned to Jerusalem and tried to join the followers of Jesus, but the churches in Judaea were frightened by him. They were skeptical when he claimed he had become a follower of Jesus. After conversing with him, however, I became convinced he was sincere in his commitment to Jesus and the good news. I undertook to bring him to our leaders in Jerusalem.[2] Eventually, they too became convinced Saul was

---

1. Acts 4:36–37.
2. Acts 9:26–30.

sincere about his newfound faith in Jesus, and they allowed him to share his views with Greek-speaking Jews in their synagogue in Jerusalem, since Greek was his main language. Alas, this did not turn out very well. He was too eager, too insistent, and too zealous! So, we shipped him off to his home region of Syria-Cilicia with a promise to stay in touch. Perhaps his witness would go better in Tarsus.

After the stoning of our beloved Stephen, various Christ followers, including some from my home region of Kupros, fled north to places like Sidon and Antioch. There they had remarkable success in sharing the good news with Greeks, including Greek-speaking Jews of the diaspora living in Antioch. The new thing was that various Gentiles, in the first place God-fearers from the synagogue there, had become Christ followers, and then pagans joined too. And this is when people there started calling us *christianoi*—partisans or devotees or followers of Christ.[3] So in fact Saul was not the first "Apostle to the Gentiles." In fact, even Simon Peter, "the apostle to the Jews," brought Cornelius and his family to our faith before any of Saul's missionary journeys.

Eventually, however, Saul came to be called the Apostle to the Gentiles. When I introduced him to Peter and the others in Jerusalem, I recounted the story of his vision of Christ and the commission that was given him. The Jerusalem leaders were quite leery of endorsing Saul. When things didn't go well in the Hellenistic Jewish synagogues, they sent him away to his native region, as I just mentioned, and they promised to stay in touch from time to time. But what they were likely thinking was "out of sight, out of mind"!

But I couldn't forget about Saul. After some years I went to Tarsus to find Saul and see if he had made progress with sharing the faith. What I found was Saul engaging in the family business, making leather products, including tents from the skin of goats. So famous was the region for making these tents that kept out the rain, that the material they were made of, goat's skin, was called *cilicium*, after the name of the region of Cilicia.

I spent a couple of days with Saul in Tarsus and found little evidence of new followers of Christ, but I learned some things about Saul. For one thing, his father and then Saul himself became Roman citizens because

---

3. This sort of label is previously known as an outsider term used for a group the label-maker is not part of. For example, there was the term *Herodianoi*—partisans of the Herods. So ironically the term "Christian" was not chosen by Christians, but was coined by outsiders, much as the term "Methodist" was disparagingly used to describe the movement the Wesley brothers started.

they had made tents for the Roman legion stationed just outside of Tarsus. For another thing, I learned that most of his family, except an aunt and an uncle, moved to Jerusalem and his sister and nephew still lived there.

In Tarsus Saul was bereft of family but free to travel and practice his trade anywhere. His skills were always in need. He made really good wineskins, sandals, leather bags, and smaller items as well. But none of this was what the exalted Christ was calling him to do. So, I suggested he come back to Antioch with me and try his hand at speaking to the Gentiles in the synagogue.

This turned out well! Saul was at his most persuasive self in various settings in Antioch, and soon the fellowship of Christ followers was growing and growing. Antioch was already a cosmopolitan city where all sorts of people mingled, and the Christ followers in Antioch, Jew and Gentile alike, had no issues with dining and meeting in each other's homes. If there were purity concerns, the stricter Jews would visit the *mikveh* after dining in a Gentile's house and that would take care of the problem. Besides, the weather was hot and the ritual baths cooled a person off.

In due course, the Antioch Christians commissioned Saul and me to take the good news abroad, and I immediately thought of going home to Kupros. Saul was amenable to the idea. At that point, having had some success in Antioch, I think he would have gone anywhere to fulfill his calling. Before we left, I convinced Saul I wanted to take my nephew, young John Mark with us. Saul was somewhat hesitant. In fact, he asked me, "Is this the young Mark that ran away from the garden of Gethsemane when Jesus was taken captive, leaving his robe behind?"[4] I admitted he was, but added he had grown up a lot since then. Saul's only reply was, "We'll see." Mark was brought along simply to be our helper. A strong lad, he carried our packs for us, which included a tent in case we needed to camp along the way.

We sailed from Seleucia, the major port near Antioch, south by southwest to the east end of Kupros. The small boat had only one sail but the journey was not long. These boats could easily sail from point to point along the coast, but in our case, it had to venture out into the ocean, the *Mare Nostrum*—"Our Sea," as the Romans say.

---

4. Mark 14:51–52.

IN THE WORDS OF BARNABAS—PAUL'S COMPANION

Sketch of a first century small sailing boat like the sort Paul would have travelled in to Cyprus and beyond.

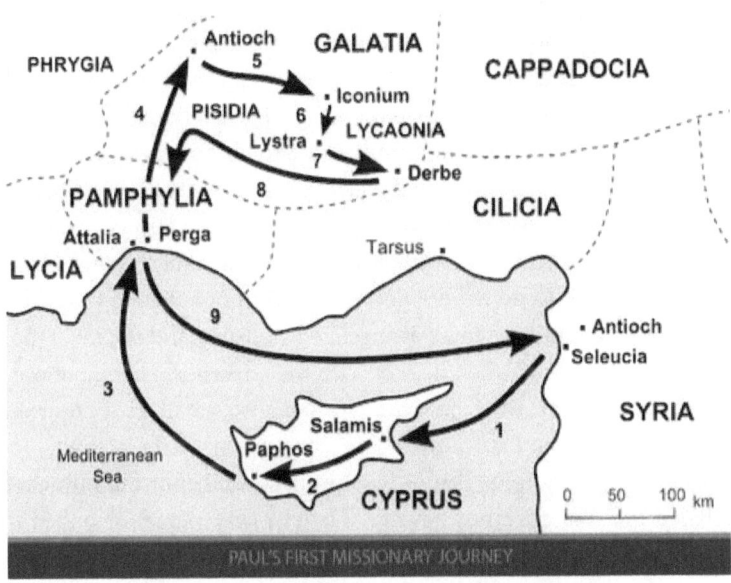

Map of Paul's first missionary journey in A.D. 48-49.

This sea journey took several days because the distance was about 148 Roman miles.[5] The normal sailing season was the Ides of March to the Ides

---

5. About 130 modern miles since a Roman mile is 0.92 of a mile. Also, the distance from Antioch to the port of Seleucia was a good forty-two miles, more than a day's

of October. Otherwise, the sea was too dangerous for travel, even for the larger grain freighters.

Our first major stop was Salamis.[6] This was the town where I grew up and I had name recognition with the leaders of that synagogue. I cannot say Saul made much of an initial positive impression, but he was not discouraged. We followed the Roman road on the south side of the island, which eventually took us to Paphos, the capital city where the Roman governor Sergius Paulus lived and ruled. Saul remembered that the heavenly vision had commissioned him to talk to governing officials, even kings. He figured that as a Roman citizen he would have a natural connection with Sergius Paulus.

It was a long walk indeed, about 155 Roman miles to reach Paphos. Our tent came in handy! Saul's plan was always to start with the synagogue. He often stressed that the good news about the Jewish messiah was quite naturally for the Jew first, and everyone else thereafter. This affected his missionary order of work.

I did not know Paphos well and the story of Saul's encounter with the governor and the court magician is a tale for another day! But one thing I want to make clear is that before Saul ever met with the governor, he already had a threefold Roman name, with Paulus being the important part used in public. It was quite impossible to simply use the soundalike name Saulos in Greek, because that had a salacious sense as an adjective—it meant to walk like a *porne*, that is, a prostitute! The Latin equivalent was hardly better. So, Paulus it was. A tale sprang up that Saul changed his name after his Damascus Road experience, but this is not true. He first used his Roman name in public when he evangelized Gentiles, and the most memorable first occasion was when he met with the governor. The name was not changed, it was simply the Latin name he had always had. From now on, he usually used the name Paul. So will I.

The visit with Sergius Paulus went well, so well after the miracle Paul performed that the governor gave us a letter of reference for our journey north back to the mainland. It turned out Sergius Paulus had family in the Roman colony city of Pisidian Antioch and Paul was keen to go there. But first we sailed to the south coast and stopped at Perga. John Mark had become restless, as young men do, and frankly not all that keen on being away from Jerusalem for so long. When he found out that we were headed

---

journey from Antioch.

6. This story is told in Acts 13.

inland, he made the unilateral decision to leave us and go home from Perga in Pamphylia. I urged him to continue with us, but he would not. Saul's only comment was "It's just as well. His heart wasn't in this from the outset. He is an impetuous young man." I was sad about this, as I had hoped to coax him along and make him into a good witness for our faith. But as it turned out, that would have to wait until much later, when he grew up a bit.

While there was a modicum of success in Perga, the journey to Pisidian Antioch in the Roman province of Galatia was an arduous one over some mountains. Yes, there were Roman roads, but there was also the danger not only from the rough terrain but also from Pisidian bandits. This was yet another mainly uphill journey of some 140 Roman miles.[7] I was getting too old for this, but not Saul. As it turned out, Pisidian Antioch was an interesting place and the letter of reference came in handy. The family members of Sergius Paulus were among the elite in that Roman colony city, and so we had an instant welcome when we produced the governor's letter.

Sergius Paulus inscription at the museum in modern Yalvaç, i.e., Pisidian Antioch.

---

7. About 120 US miles.

8. When I last visited Psidian Antioch in July 2022, the curator of the Yalvaç Museum had taken the Sergius Paulus inscription out of the courtyard and given it a safe spot inside. But someone from Ankara has misidentified the stone marker as being a sixth-century Byzantine inscription about Paul the apostle! As it happened, the mayor, the regional governor, and the curator were in the museum to celebrate the opening of a new art exhibit. I explained to the curator 1) that the inscription was not Byzantine Greek but rather an earlier Latin inscription; 2) that Sergius Paulus was a known governor of Cyprus from Paul's era who must have had family connections with Psidian Antioch; and 3) that the only reasonable explanation for why Paul and Barnabas trudged over huge mountains to get to Psidian Antioch instead of visiting cities along the coast heading towards Tarsus and eventually Antioch was because they had an endorsement to go there from the governor of Cyprus. Whether or not I convinced them, the media arrived. Meltem Çiftçi, my Turkish guide, and I were interviewed with the mayor, governor, and curator as the "discoverers of the inscription."

We waited until the sabbath since Paul was invited to speak there after the reading of the Law and the Prophets. Naturally, in a rather isolated town like Pisidian Antioch there was curiosity about this out-of-town speaker. The leaders of the synagogue said to us, "Brothers, if you have a *logos protreptikos* for us, please share."[9] Fortunately, it is now recorded in Luke's account in his Acts!

Paul then said, "Fellow Israelites and you Gentiles who worship God, listen to me! The God of the people of Israel chose our ancestors; he made the people prosper during their stay in Egypt; with mighty power he led them out of that country; for about forty years, he endured their conduct in the wilderness; and he overthrew seven nations in Canaan, giving their land to his people as their inheritance. All this took about 450 years. After this, God gave them judges until the time of Samuel the prophet. Then the people asked for a king, and he gave them Saul son of Kish, of the tribe of Benjamin, who ruled forty years. After removing Saul, he made David their king. God testified concerning him: 'I have found David son of Jesse, a man after my own heart; he will do everything I want him to do.'"

"From this man's descendants God has brought to Israel the Savior Jesus, as he promised. Before the coming of Jesus, John preached repentance and baptism to all the people of Israel. As John was completing his work, he said: 'Who do you suppose I am? I am not the one you are looking for. But there is one coming after me whose sandals I am not worthy to untie.'"

"Fellow children of Abraham and you God-fearing Gentiles, it is to us that this message of salvation has been sent. The people of Jerusalem and their rulers did not recognize Jesus, yet in condemning him they fulfilled the words of the prophets that are read every Sabbath. Though they found no proper ground for a death sentence, they asked Pilate to have him executed. When they had carried out all that was written about him, they took him down from the cross and laid him in a tomb. But God raised him from the dead and for many days he was seen by those who had traveled with him from Galilee to Jerusalem. They are now his witnesses to our people."

"We tell you the good news: What God promised our ancestors he has fulfilled for us, their children, by raising up Jesus. As it is written in the Second Psalm: 'You are my son; today I have become your father.' God raised him from the dead so that he will never be subject to decay. As God has said, 'I will give you the holy and sure blessings promised to David.'"

---

9. That is, a word of ethical exhortation. Sermons in synagogues seem to have been like the material we find in the Letter of James, primarily focused on ethics and praxis.

"So, it is also stated elsewhere: 'You will not let your holy one see decay.' Now when David had served God's purpose in his own generation, he fell asleep; he was buried with his ancestors and his body decayed. But the one whom God raised from the dead did not see decay."

"Therefore, my friends, I want you to know that through Jesus the forgiveness of sins is proclaimed to you. Through him everyone who believes is set free from *every* sin, a justification you were not able to obtain under the law of Moses. Take care that what the prophets have said does not happen to you: 'Look, you scoffers, wonder and perish, for I am going to do something in your days that you would never believe, even if someone told you.'"[10]

I was apprehensive as to how the congregation would react to this sermon, but they were surprisingly positive and invited Saul to come and speak again the following sabbath. Not only so, but they followed him out of the synagogue asking questions and sharing thoughts.

The second time around he was not as well received. At first things looked good as a large portion of the town came to hear the proclamation; in fact, he had to share his message outdoors and many Gentiles from the city were present. This angered some of the Jews who began to contradict Paul's teaching with vehemence, but both Paul and I had to answer them in strong terms and said: "We had to speak the word of God to you first. Since you reject it and do not consider yourselves worthy of eternal life, we now turn to the Gentiles. For this is what the Lord has commanded us: 'I have made you a light for the Gentiles, that you may bring salvation to the ends of the earth.'"[11]

The end result of all this is that a good number of Gentiles accepted the message about Christ and they shared it with others in the region. The Jewish leaders, however, stirred up some of the elite God-fearers or synagogue adherents, both men and women, and they ran us out of town! We shook the dust off our feet and moved on down the Roman road to Iconium.[12]

Iconium is an interesting city. It had recently been renamed *Claudiconium*, in an effort to flatter the emperor Claudius and get patronage for the city. Our reception in this city was better in terms of length than in

---

10. This is the longest of the missionary speeches by Paul and is meant to provide the example for how he exhorted in the synagogue. This follows the NIV text in Acts 13. Notice that the quotations are from the LXX of Psalm 2:7; Isaiah 55:3; Psalm 16:10 (see Septuagint); and Hab 1:5.

11. Here the quotation is from Isaiah 49:6.

12. A ninety-five-mile walk in modern miles.

Pisidian Antioch. Both Jews and Greeks believed in such numbers that the outcome became too evident to those who opposed such religious changes. Partly the response was so strong because there were several miracles that happened while we were there proclaiming the good news. We had enough support that when there were plans to stone us some of the new converts warned us! We got out of town just in time and headed to Lystra. Here again the response was different.

Lystra is in old Lyconia and the Lystrans speak their own language, neither Greek nor Latin really. When we got there, they understood us, but we couldn't understand them unless they spoke Greek. Nevertheless, the response to the good news in Greek, when accompanied by a miraculous healing of a lame man, produced an enormous response. As we learned later, they suddenly thought we were Zeus and Hermes! I suppose I was seen as Zeus due to my age and long beard, and Paul as Hermes, the messenger of the gods, since he did the proclaiming.

The legend was that Zeus and Hermes visited the city in the disguise of human beings and no one received them or showed them hospitality except a poor, elderly couple named Baucis and Philemon.[13] The gods in gratitude greatly blessed the couple, and the city thereafter vowed not to let the gods come and go again without a proper reception. So, once the healed lame man stood up, this produced a huge shock of recognition, and the next thing we knew they were carrying us around on their shoulders! Then, they proceeded to get the ceremonial bull to offer sacrifice to us!

With alarm it finally dawned on us what was happening. Paul held up his hand to the crowd to be quiet. He said to them, "Friends, why are you doing this? We too are only human, like you. We are bringing you good news, telling you to turn from these worthless things to the living God, who made the heavens and the earth and the sea and everything in them. In the past, he let all nations go their own way. Yet he has not left himself without a witness: he has shown kindness by giving you rain from heaven and crops in their seasons; he provides you with plenty of food and fills your hearts with joy."

This speech barely slowed down their enthusiastic response, but at that very juncture Jews from both Pisidian Antioch and Iconium arrived, saying we were frauds and charlatans! Somehow they convinced a number of people to join them in stoning us, especially Paul! He was dragged

---

13. This tale is found in Ovid's *Metamorphosis*. See the discussion in my *Acts of the Apostles* (1996).

IN THE WORDS OF BARNABAS—PAUL'S COMPANION

outside the city but, fortunately, the new converts came to his aid and he returned to finish speaking to them, despite his bruises.

The next morning, we left for Derbe, a small city just beyond the border of the Galatian province, not far from Lystra. As we were going there, I suggested we stop and head for the coast. After all, much had already been accomplished, but Paul was silent and continued to walk towards Derbe, about fifty Roman miles farther down the road. I mumbled, "Well, let's hope the stones are softer in Derbe." Paul just smiled and kept going. He was indeed a man of great courage coupled with great conviction. It was hard not to admire his perseverance, even in the face of strong opposition. We did not have much of a reception in little Derbe, so we turned around and went back through the three cities we had just come from in Galatia to strengthen and confirm the fledgling converts God's grace had created in those places. Paul was wise enough to appoint leaders, which he called elders, in each place, so the work could be further consolidated.

Finally, after many months, we made our way back to the coast, preached once more in Perga, bordered a boat in Attalia and sailed back to Syrian Antioch with much to tell for our troubles. While we may have thought that we had left controversy behind, alas it was not so. In our absence, Peter himself had come to check out the reports of a growing number of house churches in Antioch. When we arrived Peter was enjoying a banquet in the house of one of the new Gentile converts, that is until some men came from Jacob[14] and made a huge objection to Peter's behavior, saying Jacob would never approve of such banqueting with the unclean, eating unclean food! Peter was shocked; he had not thought this was a problem until then. I have to confess, to my shame, that I too withdrew from such fellowship for a time, thinking Jacob must have given these men specific orders about such a matter. Fortunately, the matter was eventually resolved in Jerusalem,[15] but not until the middle of the century. I had never seen Paul so angry, before or thereafter. He accused Peter—and me too—of hypocrisy!

Only later did I realize that these men were Judaizers—Pharisaic followers of Jesus who were strict about Torah observances and thought

---

14. The Jewish name for James in the New Testament is Jacob, after the patriarch. In this case we are referring to the brother of Jesus who had become one of the leaders of the Jerusalem church. Paul tells us in 1 Corinthians 15 that the probable reason this happened (since he was never a disciple of Jesus during Jesus' lifetime)is that Jesus appeared to his brother Jacob and commissioned him.

15. See Acts 15.

everyone had to convert to Judaism to follow Jesus. After harassing the converts in Antioch, they went on to Galatia to get the newly won converts there to commit to keeping the whole Mosaic covenant—all 613 commandments!

Some weeks later when these men left, Paul resolved to return to his new converts in Galatia to make sure they had not wavered. Before going he wrote them a now famous letter, trying to head off his Gentile converts from accepting circumcision and all that went with it. I spoke to Paul about going with him and mentioned taking Mark again with us, but he would hear none of it. He was happy for me, but not Mark, to join him. It occurred to me that he had no plans to go to Cyprus, so I suggested I would return there with Mark to strengthen the new disciples there. He readily agreed to this. In the end Paul went back to Galatia with Silvanus and later Timothy.

I have some regrets for how these things turned out, but I had seen promise in young Mark. Later, Peter came to see this promise too. Later yet, Paul and Mark were reconciled. As for me, I continued to work in my homeland with much success, but I'm an old man now! I am thankful for all that. What I just learned, which prompted these reflections, was the news of the martyrdom of the Apostle to the Gentiles. Paul was beheaded in Rome near what is likely to be the end of the reign of terror by Nero. And I hear Peter, who is also in Rome, is in danger of death too. Nero blamed "the Way" for the fire in Rome and it led to numerous deaths of Christ's followers. Some were even set alight in the Circus Maximus, they say.

At my age I do not fear death. I have lived passed the three score and ten Torah refers to as a good old age. And I have no worries about our movement dying out. Jesus the Messiah will not let that happen! For now, I am a thankful old man, grateful to have played a part in the life of Paul and in the spreading the good news about the life, death and resurrection of Jesus.

IN THE WORDS OF JOHN MARK—
PAUL'S OFF-AND-ON FRIEND

John Mark, like other Jews, had both a Jewish name, John, and a Greco-Roman name, Mark. From Acts 12 and 13 we learn that John Mark's mother, Mary, had a home in Jerusalem. Since the strange story of a "young man" fleeing nearly naked when Jesus was arrested appears only in the Gospel of Mark, many believe he is the same man who wrote the Gospel. He probably followed from afar and then ran back to his home that fateful night. Later we find him traveling with Saul/Paul and Barnabas who, as an older man, was probably his uncle. John Mark certainly traveled on the first missionary journey to Cyprus and then Perga, but he returned to Jerusalem at that point. Barnabas wanted to take John Mark on another journey, but Paul said no. So, Barnabas took Mark back to his home in Cyprus. We never hear from Barnabas after that. But I'm confident this same John Mark is the author of the Gospel according to Mark, our first and shortest Gospel.

St. Mark (John Mark) by Franz Hals (c. 1582–1666). Painted c. 1625–1630.

Yes, it's true. When I was young, I was impetuous, stubborn, and often scared. Sometimes my curiosity overcame my fears. It was me who followed behind Jesus and his disciples as they walked to the garden of Gethsemane. It was also me who ran off from the garden when a soldier grabbed my robe as Jesus was arrested. I was a young lad at the time, and all those soldiers, temple police, and Romans frightened me badly. It took me a while to live down the stories about the youth that fled from Jesus nearly naked. Fortunately, I didn't have far to run since my parents had a house in Jerusalem, within the old city walls.[1] My father died of some sort of pestilence when I was in my twenties. I became the man of the house but it was run by my dear mother, Miriam. In due course our home became a meeting place for the followers of Jesus, one of the first such places after the early meetings in the "upper room." Our home had a gated entrance and servants to help us, including Rhoda, but that's a story for another day.

Barnabas, my uncle and a Levite, mentored me after my father died and made sure I got a decent education, including learning Greek. I have to admit though that I was not a scholar! My Greek, especially my written Greek, betrayed the fact that I was normally thinking in Aramaic even when I was writing in Greek![2] As I am writing this now, I've just finished my good news about Jesus *bios* reflecting on the testimonies of Peter, which I believe is the first such account in Greek to appear. Doubtless there will be more.[3] In some ways, I have lived to see the end of an era. Paul was executed earlier in this decade and then Peter was crucified. These two men were, humanly speaking, most responsible for the spread of the Jesus movement in the last thirty-some years. I was only their companion and helper at various points.

The first opportunity I had to get involved in the movement was in my early twenties, when Uncle Barnabas invited me to come along on a missionary trip from Antioch. Saul of Tarsus, the same Saul who had persecuted Jesus' followers in Jerusalem, went with us! I was in awe of Saul. My mother did not want me to go. She did not trust this new "turncoat," as she called him, but Barnabas persuaded her that Saul's change of heart was real.

I suppose I saw this whole expedition as an opportunity to get out of town and have a big adventure. Jerusalem had been the only world I knew growing up, and I longed to see what else was out there. Barnabas told tales

---

1. On which see Acts 12:12.

2. On which see the introduction to my commentary on the *Gospel of Mark* (2001).

3. On the Gospels as biographies of an ancient sort, see R. Burridge, *What are the Gospels?* (2020). See also Craig Keener, *Christobiography* (2019).

about growing up on Kupros and I romanticized some of what he said. But as the youngest and strongest, I became the baggage boy on long walks from Salamis to Paphos. Traveling turned out to be a lot of hard work, carrying a tent, supplies, extra sandals, wineskins, and so much more!

I have to admit that Paphos and the strange encounter with the sorcerer Elymas was interesting, to say the least. It's hard to tell the difference between a charlatan and someone who is actually drawing on some dark power to obtain things he wants from unsuspecting people, including authorities. Whatever was the case, Saul took care of him. As a result, Governor Sergius Paulus granted us some help for the next stage of our mission. In fact, his help changed the itinerary of the mission. And here was the first time I heard Saul identify himself by his Greek or Latin names—Paulos or Paulus.[4] From now on, I too will call him Paul.

When we got back to the coast of the mainland near Attalia, we went to the ancient city of Perga first. Here we met with some success in making disciples of Jesus. But when I heard Paul and Barnabas talking about trekking through very dangerous, mountainous terrain into the province of Galatia and to Pisidian Antioch, I quit! The prospect of fending off Pisidian bandits at every twist and turn in the Roman road while climbing a mountain with a heavy pack was not only unappealing but also scared me to death! Furthermore, there were reports of disease as well in the region. So, not without some regret, I told Uncle Barnabas I was booking passage to go back home to Jerusalem while we were still on the coast. Not for me the Herculean form of discipleship that seemed to only excite Paul to further adventures. I later regretted this somewhat impetuous but also somewhat rational decision.

I arrived back in Judaea after a week of going from one port to the next on small sailing boats until I got to Herod's spectacular man-made port of Caesarea Maritima. From there I walked back up to that "city set on a hill," where I found Jerusalem in disarray. For one thing, there was a food shortage. For another, the widows who followed Jesus had been cut off from the local dole due to increasing animosity against "the Way." My sweet mother was working hard to remedy that problem. Just after I arrived, the apostles Peter and John were dragged before the Sanhedrin and thrown into jail! But thanks to divine intervention, they

---

4. See Acts 13:9. There was no name change as a result of the Damascus Road experience. In fact, there wasn't really a name change. Saul simply used his preexisting Greek and Roman names when speaking with a Roman authority.

miraculously escaped.⁵ They reported all this to those meeting in my mother's house, and then Peter disappeared to foreign parts to evangelize primarily Jews. He would not return for quite some time. The church in Jerusalem was undergoing both persecution and the occasional prosecution thanks to both King Herod Agrippa and members of the Sanhedrin who had approved the stoning of Stephen. While I assumed that when I returned to Jerusalem things would be more peaceful and less dangerous, I was wrong! So, when Barnabas got in touch with me by messenger upon his return to Antioch with news of the success of the mission in Galatia, I was open to rejoining him and Paul on further missions.

Paul, however, was having none of it. He and Barnabas argued about this for some while and could not come to any agreement. There was also the further problem that some of the Pharisaic Jewish followers of Jesus had gone to Antioch and pressured Peter and Barnabas to stop eating with Gentiles in Gentile homes. Paul accused them of giving in to pressure instead of standing on principle. As a result, Paul went overland to Galatia taking Silvanus with him and later recruiting Timothy.

So, I went with Barnabas once again to Kupros. We struggled, but our years there were not entirely fruitless. Meanwhile, we got all these reports from Antioch about Paul's expanding mission to Gentiles and how it was heading west to Asia Minor, Macedonia, Greece, and elsewhere. Simon Peter as well was somewhere in Bithynia and beyond. None of us saw him again until we all came back to Jerusalem for the Council to decide on the proper approach to integrating Gentiles into the Jesus movement.

The thing that surprised me most about the Jerusalem Council was how Peter stood up for Paul's mission. He championed the notion that Gentiles didn't have to become either Jews or even God-fearers and synagogue adherents to be part of the Way. But would this mean there would be two churches—a more Jewish one and a more Gentile one? No one was in favor of that either.

The matter stalled until Jacob cleared his throat and spoke out. While he himself was going to continue to be an observant Jew, he did not think this option should be imposed on Gentile converts. He made a decree that going forward Gentiles must avoid going to pagan temples, in particular pagan dinner parties where pagan deities were honored and even thought

---

5. While this story is told in Acts 12, Luke's account is not strictly chronological. Rather he places stories about major figures like Peter together in a series of passages. In this passage, Peter's story in Acts ends except for a cameo appearance at the Jerusalem Council in Acts 15, which took place c. AD 50.

to be present. Jacob said they must avoid idolatry and the sort of immorality that happened after men drank too much at such pagan feasts. This meant avoiding 1) *eidolothuton,* literally meat sacrificed to idols and offered to that supposed deity at such temple dinner parties; 2) animals, like birds, that were strangled and cooked for the dinner; 3) blood in the meat; and 4) sexual immorality, which was also common at these occasions. In short, he banned the converts from going to dinner parties at pagan temples where one would find all four of those repulsive things. It really was more about the venue than the menu.

In the decree, Jacob mentioned that this would provide a better witness to Jews in the synagogue who associated those temples and feasts with a violation of the heart of the Mosaic law. After all, the Ten Commandments ban idolatry and immorality! This compromise seemed amenable to all except the Pharisaic hardliners in the Jerusalem church, and later Saul would implement the decree banning temple feast participation in Corinth.[6] But what were the implications of the decree? To me it meant that Jews and Gentiles, if they were to meet, eat, fellowship and worship together, would now be a part of not just another Jewish sect or movement, but a new religious reality. Now Jew and Gentile would be united in Christ, not Jew and Gentile united in the synagogue. I came to this conclusion gradually, but it was clear that Paul had already seen these implications of the good news, that salvation would be by grace through faith in the death and resurrection of Jesus and adherence to a new covenant, not a mere renewal of the Mosaic covenant—though some commandments of the Mosaic law were reaffirmed in the new covenant.[7]

After that mid-century crucial meeting, I did not see Simon Peter again for many years. My mother died in Jerusalem not long after the Jerusalem Council, and there really was nothing tying me to the city thereafter. I returned first to Kupros and heard about how the Jesus movement was making headway even in Rome, even without apostles there to lead it. In fact, there began to be a presence of Jesus followers in Rome after Pentecost when some converts returned to the so-called Eternal City with newfound faith in Jesus. So, eventually I made my way to Rome, as did Peter in the early 60s. Paul was already there under house arrest awaiting trial before Nero. I resolved to be of whatever help I could be to these two men. No one could have foreseen the great fire in Rome. No one was expecting Nero

---

6. See 1 Cor 8–10.

7. See Gal 3–4, in Paul's earliest letter.

to blame the followers of Christ, making them scapegoats for something they didn't do. Before that happened, Paul was released from house arrest because the Jewish authorities did not show up to accuse him at his trial. As a Roman citizen Paul's case was dismissed. He thereafter returned to help Timothy and Titus in Ephesus and elsewhere.

Meanwhile, Peter was writing letters to his various converts in Bithynia, Pontus, and elsewhere with the aid of Silvanus, whose Greek was excellent. I for my part persuaded Peter to let me take down his memoirs, especially his memories of the early preaching and healing ministry of Jesus. Peter's Greek was never very good, so basically I translated his Aramaic into better Greek. It was a long and arduous process. Only after his martyrdom by crucifixion was I able to finally finish my good news account based on his testimony.

Meanwhile, Paul was retaken by the Roman authorities after the fire in Rome, as Nero needed to find some "infamous" Christ followers to blame. I had gone across to *Ephesos* to help Timothy with some difficulties there. Happily, Paul had asked Timothy to come to him while he was in the Mamertine prison and to bring Mark, "as he is useful to me." I am thankful we were finally reunited and reconciled before Paul was executed.

Now, I am alone in Rome, approaching old age. With Peter and Paul and others gone on to glory, I am not sure what God would have me do next. I pray regularly that I may be faithful to the Lord unto death. I would like to be able to say as Paul did in his last letter, "I have fought the good fight, I have run the race, and I have kept the faith."[8] May it be so for me too, by the grace of God.

---

8. 2 Tim 4:7.

IN THE WORDS OF SILAS / SILVANUS—PAUL'S SECOND JOURNEY COMPANION

Silas is first mentioned in Acts 15:22. He was considered a leader, a prophet, and a good speaker, all traits that Paul admired. When the Council of Jerusalem ended, he and Judas Barsabbas were asked to join Paul and Barnabas as they journeyed back to Antioch. There Paul planned his second missionary journey, but he and Barnabas argued over whether to include Mark. So, Silas went with Paul instead. While they were in Philippi, both were imprisoned. A "convenient" earthquake broke their chains (Acts 16). This is why the apostle Silas is shown carrying a broken chain! Like Saul, Silas had a Roman name, Silvanus ("of the forest"). Silas can be found in the book of Acts, 2 Corinthians, 1 and 2 Thessalonians, and 1 Peter, where he is called "a faithful brother."

Modern icon painting of Silas done in the workshop in Meteora that my tour group visited.

Like Mark I worked with both Paul and Peter, the difference being, I did it on an ongoing basis during Paul's second missionary journey and then helped him with his first letters to Christ followers in Thessaloniki. But that was only possible because Jacob had appointed me, along with Judas Barsabbas (not Iscariot) to accompany Paul on his travels to explain the decree to his Gentile converts.¹ Greek actually is my native language, so there were no translation issues whenever I addressed these new Christ followers who also spoke Greek. I had been one of the leaders in the Hellenistic synagogue in Jerusalem before becoming a follower of the Christ, and thereafter was a leader among the Greek-speaking Jewish followers of the Christ. Jacob, brother of Jesus and now leader of us all in Jerusalem, knew me well for many years, and so the appointment to go and read out the decree while traveling with Saul was neither a surprise nor a burden.

Paul and I began our travels from Antioch, crossing the province of Galatia and visiting the Christ followers in Lystra, Iconium, and Pisidian Antioch. This journey would take us on to Macedonia and then Greece. Along the way we picked up Timothy, who was from Lystra. His father was Greek, but his mother was a Jew who had become a Christ follower even before Timothy. Paul made it a regular practice on his journeys to go to the synagogues first. As he liked to say, "The good news is for the Jew first!"² Consequently, Paul decided after much consideration and prayer to circumcise Timothy, so there would be no questions about our "Jewishness" in regard to any of the three of us. We were Jews who had observant Jewish parents before we became Christ followers. This allowed our ministry to those in the synagogue to go forward without any initial roadblocks.

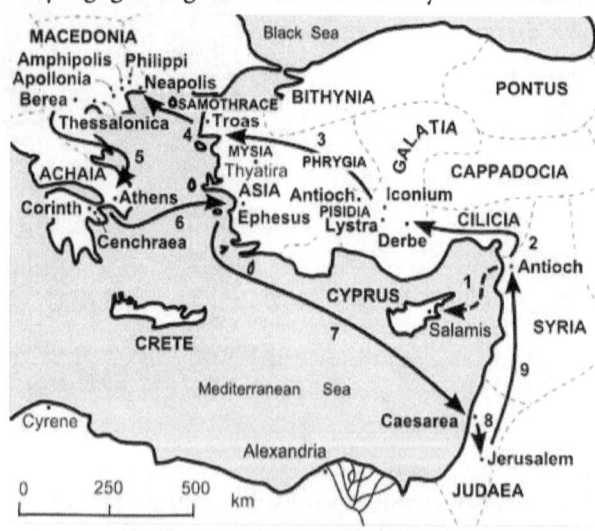

The second missionary journey of Paul.

1. Acts 15:22.

2. See Rom 1:16. The notion that Paul only attempted to convert Gentiles and Peter only Jews is of course false. It was just that Paul's primary focus was on bringing Gentiles to the faith, and Peter's on Jews.

IN THE WORDS OF SILAS / SILVANUS

While I was still with Paul in Galatia he was determined to get to Ephesus no matter what. He thought it would be a promising place to plant the faith, not least because it was already religiously diverse. But as we were traveling from Galatia, Paul got one of those messages from above. He said the Holy Spirit prevented him from going straight to Ephesus, and instead diverted him to the north. When we came to the border of Mesia and Bithynia the Spirit diverted him again, and we went on to Alexander Troas, near the coast. While there Paul had a night vision of a person from Macedonia asking him to come across the Hellespont and share the good news. As for me, God has not given me voices or visions. I have strong faith in God, but no voices or visions! So, I had to just take Paul's word for it and, as things turned out, God blessed our efforts.[3] Furthermore, the man from Macedonia turned out to be an itinerant doctor named Luke, who lived in Philippi but regularly traveled back and forth from Philippi to Troas.[4] He was to become very important to Paul later as Paul's eyesight began to deteriorate. What did not deteriorate was Paul's determination to spread the good news and reach as many Jews and Gentiles as humanly possible. Sometimes I wondered where all that energy and commitment came from but, of course, it was ultimately from God's Spirit.

In Philippi, Luke gave Paul eye ointment or balm of some kind. It was actually while we were in Philippi that Luke became a genuine follower of Christ, and came to be called one of Paul's partners, a true yokefellow who later would help resolve difficulties in that city when Paul couldn't be there. For instance, Luke was very helpful when two of the female leaders and co-workers there, Euodia and Syntyche, had some serious disagreements.

About the incident in the jail in Philippi . . .[5] To say the least it had some surprising aspects. Paul was not in the least worried about being there, unlike me, but he tried to cheer me up by leading us in singing some Psalms. He had a strong, low singing voice, and I had a higher voice so we sang well together, though the other inmates in the cell didn't appreciate it going on late into the night. And then the earthquake hit! I suppose the locals would say that Tyche, the god of luck, was with us. We were not hurt, but the door to the jail broke open! We could have bolted, but Saul said no,

---

3. See Acts 16:6–10.

4. A parallel can be drawn here with Galen from a slightly later time, who traveled between his home base in Pergamon and Rome practicing medicine. Good physicians were in demand, and various of them itinerated.

5. See Acts 16.

someone will come to check on us. It turned out to be the jailer, who was shaking as much as the earth did! He was afraid his charges had escaped, but Saul reassured him no one had made a run for it.

Yet another surprise—the jailer asked us, "How can I and my family be saved?" I thought he was referring to being rescued from the aftershocks of the earthquake. Paul, however, missing no opportunity, shared the gospel of a different sort of salvation with him. He embraced the Way believing that Jesus was truly God and that he had saved Paul and our fellow prisoners from death.

And then there was the Roman city official, one of the *duumviri*,[6] who came and asked us to leave Philippi, thinking Paul and I were bad luck and had brought the earthquake on them. He told us never to come back. Paul however said, "I'm a Roman citizen, with right to trial before any punishment including incarceration so, we will sit here until we receive an apology!" An apology! I just about fell over when he said that. Either Paul was the bravest person I've ever met, or the one with the most hubris or perhaps self-confidence. The official looked at Paul's Roman diptych,[7] which he carried verifying his Roman citizenship, then turned pale, mumbled some regrets, and we left the jail. We did not promise that we would not return!

Despite all this excitement, for me the most interesting stop was further south in Thessaloniki, the city named after Alexander's sister, a thoroughly Greek rather than Roman city. In some ways, the Romans were more tolerant of multiple deities and religions than the Greeks of Macedonia. Sadly, several Christ followers lost their lives trying to protect us in Thessaloniki. They helped us get out of town before things got worse. What triggered the strong reaction was that various high-status women became followers of Christ through Paul's preaching. One thing I will say about Paul, he was irrepressible. No matter what happened, no matter what went wrong, he had so much faith in Christ and belief in his calling that he just wouldn't give up, despite persecution, despite jailing, despite being stoned

---

6. Because Philippi was a Roman colony city, it was mainly governed by two military officials (hence *duumviri*) appointed directly by Rome. A Greek city had been turned into a Roman colony city as a retirement place for mustered-out Roman soldiers. The city had also been renamed in honor of the old Emperor—*Colonia Augusta Iulia Philippensis*—after Octavian had been named emperor by the Senate in 27 BC. Its law was the same as the law of the city of Rome. The Romans there were among the elites in the city who served as mayors, city treasurers, and the like.

7. A Roman citizen had a small identity card, sometimes made of wood that folded like a wallet, and was called a diptych. The term more broadly was used of a bifold writing tablet.

IN THE WORDS OF SILAS / SILVANUS

by his fellow Jews, and despite being a "wanted" man, and not in a good way. His way of dealing with this pressure was to stay in a place as long as he could, but when the situation began to endanger the infant congregations, then he would go on to the next place.

Finally, I would like to share with you about the letters Timothy and I helped Paul write to the Thessalonians. Paul was worried about the Thessalonians for two reasons: 1) he had to leave town before he was sure that the ongoing existence of the community of faith was not in doubt; and 2) the Thessalonians were badly traumatized by the loss of some of their fellow believers due to persecution. They even wondered if those who had died were going to miss out on the end times and the return of Christ. What was to happen to them now that they were dead?

Paul decided to take a pastoral approach in his first letter to the Thessalonians. Thus, Paul spoke to them in a manner they would be familiar with, following classic funeral speeches, a major part of epideictic rhetoric.[8] Timothy and I agreed with this approach. Later we returned to Thessaloniki to check on the new Christ followers and deliver this letter of comfort and consolation. Paul emphasized that God himself would deal with persecutors but, more importantly, he reassured the converts that the deceased would benefit from the return of Christ; in fact, they would be some of the first to be raised from the dead. They will be among the first to greet the Lord's return, meeting him in the air, and then returning with him to earth to reign with him. That was quite a promise, a powerful piece of rhetorical consolation to say the least!

Paul traveled on to Athens while we went back to Thessaloniki to strengthen the new congregation and his letter had the desired effect. While Timothy and I helped with the forming of that letter, the substance was all Paul's. We simply agreed with it and pronounced the Amen!

Working with Paul was challenging, not least because he did not shy from controversy, whether in the synagogue or the agora. While he didn't deliberately provoke controversy, it seemed to follow him around. Later, when we got back together in Corinth and all three of us, Timothy included, preached there,[9] Paul recounted for me some of his misadventures I had not

---

8. Epideictic is the rhetoric of praise and blame, and at funerals usually just praise was expressed. Epideictic rhetoric is not providing arguments but rather laudatory statements about the deceased and comfort for the living.

9. 2 Cor 1:19.

witnessed. Comparing himself to other so-called apostles who had come through Corinth and entertained the Corinthians, he said,

> Are they servants of Christ? . . . I am more. I have worked much harder, been in prison more frequently, been flogged more severely, and been exposed to death again and again. Five times I received from the Jews the forty lashes minus one. Three times I was beaten with rods, once I was pelted with stones, three times I was shipwrecked, I spent a night and a day in the open sea, I have been constantly on the move. I have been in danger from rivers, in danger from bandits, in danger from my fellow Jews, in danger from Gentiles; in danger in the city, in danger in the country, in danger at sea; and in danger from false believers. I have labored and toiled and have often gone without sleep; I have known hunger and thirst and have often gone without food; I have been cold and naked."[10]

This misery list I do not think involves exaggeration. One had to put on "the full armor of Christ," as Paul used to say, to travel and minister with him.

There is so much more I could say about Paul, but I would be remiss not to say something about what has happened to me since Paul's second missionary adventures. I eventually went on to Rome, as one of Paul's advance guard. He would arrive in due course. Actually, he didn't get to Rome for three or so more years after me, because he had returned to Jerusalem, caused a near riot in the temple, was taken prisoner by the authorities and languished under house arrest. Fortunately, he had his physician Luke with him. It was about ten years after the Jerusalem Council that he finally arrived in Rome, chained to a Roman soldier. Still undaunted, while under house arrest he tried to convert one Roman soldier after another who was chained to him for the day. I guess you could say he had a captive audience—one could ask who was really the captive in this case.

As for me, I was glad to hear that he was released because the Jewish authorities never came to press charges against the Roman citizen Paul. I did not return with him to the East, to Ephesus, where Timothy was doing his best to nurture the infant house churches there and elsewhere in Asia Minor. Instead, when Simon Peter finally arrived from Bithynia I helped him with various tasks, including the writing of his missive to various house churches he established all over the northern part of Asia Minor and

---

10. 2 Cor 11:23–27.

beyond into northern Galatia, Pontus, and elsewhere. I finally found out where he had disappeared to after the Jerusalem Council, and he certainly had not been idle.[11] There is more to tell about Paul and Simon Peter, but I will leave that task to others. I continue to live out my days in Rome, with fellow Christ followers such as Priscilla.[12] Many of us have grown old here, and in some cases it has more to do with the miles and adventures lived through, than just the passing of the years. I am thankful for my time with both of the great apostles who spread the good news west from Jerusalem to Rome, but am sad to have lived long enough to see them both executed by the Romans. In a human sense, they were irreplaceable, but their deaths not only did not stifle the gospel, their bravery in face of persecution, prosecution, and execution actually has helped spread it.[13] But why should we be surprised by this, when the movement actually started in earnest by the death and resurrection of Christ? Or, as Paul once said, "A seed must fall into the ground and die before it can rise up to a new form of life."[14]

---

11. See 1 Pet 5:12–13. It seems clear that Silas is credited with writing the document itself. Notice as well that it is written from Rome, here called Babylon, Christian code language for the Eternal City (see Rev 18).

12. See my *Priscilla, the Life of an Early Christian* (2019).

13. See the later comment of Tertullian—"Plures efficimur, quotiens metimur a vobis: semen est sanguis Christianorum," which has been loosely translated as "the blood of the martyrs is the seed of the Church" (*Apologeticus*, L.13). Literally, what the Latin says is "We multiply when you reap us. The blood of the Christians is seed."

14. See 1 Cor 15:36–38.

IN THE WORDS OF EUODIA— ONE OF PAUL'S MANY CONVERTS

Euodia, aka Lydia, was a lady from the town of Thyatira in the region of Lydia in the western part of what is Turkey today. At that time, Thyatira was probably a Roman settlement, notable for all its trades, including the production of expensive purple dye. According to Acts 16, she gave hospitality to Paul, Silas, and Timothy as they were passing through Philippi. She was in charge of the house. As a reputable businesswoman (and probably a widow) she was well to do. All accounts suggest she specialized in cloth dyed purple, a royal color. As a Jew or a God-fearer (probably the latter), she would have been comfortable speaking with Paul and his other Jewish friends. As a woman inviting men into her home, she was probably a widow, an exceptionally wealthy woman with servants. Regardless, this woman of Lydia, was unique.

Painting of Lydia found in the small chapel at the archaeological site of Philippi.

IN THE WORDS OF EUODIA

Many people call me Lydia, not Euodia! Some just refer to me as "the Lydian," since I am from that region in western Asia Minor. This region had its own culture and language. Of course, I am also fluent in Latin and Greek. In particular I came from Thyatira, a town well known for its many trades, not the least part of which was our dying industry. We processed various shades of cloth used in the making of garments for the elite, especially the rulers. Emperors highly valued our red and red-purple cloth.

Where I come from matters as this is where I gained my skills and trade in the art of dying cloth. In Lydia, being far from the sea, we do not usually make our purple dye from the secretions of the various types of sea snails collectively called murex shells. It's simply too hard and too expensive to coax dyes from snails! We get our various shades of dyes from the madder root (*Rubia*), which can be grown here abundantly.

 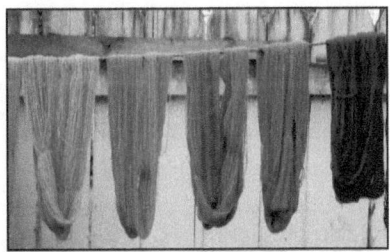

The madder root in a basket, and then yarn died various shades of red and purple using the color that comes from the madder root.

Our family business prospered in producing such garments during this century, which has seen more and more Roman prefects, procurators, centurions, and even emperors wanting garments with such bold colors. We moved to Philippi and our business continued to thrive. Now I am a widow, sad to say, but a very successful businesswoman. Praise God!

Previously I was involved in the faith of the Jewish people. However, my life took a turn in a different direction the day I met Paul, Silas, and Timothy. How this came about is certainly interesting! I was at a prayer meeting at the Strymon River with fellow Jews and God-fearers, including several servants from my household. The Jewish population in this Roman colony city is not large enough to have a quorum, which in any case had to be a certain number of *men* to organize and build a synagogue, so we met by this stream on the sabbath. In fact, it was only women at this meeting. I looked up from praying and there standing before me were four men—three strangers and Luke the physician, whom I already knew. Luke said that Paul would like to address us and we were happy to have him do so.

ENCOUNTERS WITH PAUL

I had never heard this message about Jesus before! Somehow, God opened my heart to Paul's message, which dealt with some of my deepest longings and anxieties about many things. I worry about what the future holds for Jewish or God-fearing persons like myself who are constantly under pressure and ridicule from various sorts of pagans. I worry about how our women are treated, especially successful literate women like myself. But Paul's message explained that it didn't matter if you were Jew or Gentile, slave or free, married or single in order to be a saved person, a person set free and reconciled fully to God through Jesus of Nazareth. So, I not only heard the message but also embraced and believed it! The next thing you know Paul was baptizing me and various of my servants right there in the River Styron.

My immediate response was to invite these visitors to stay in my house. I said, "If you now consider me a believer, then accept my hospitality and come stay in my house. There is plenty of room."[1] Thus began a long, positive relationship with those spreading the good news about Jesus. I continued to support Paul and his work and my house became the place where the good news took root in Philippi. Before long there would be other houses that provided venues for worship and fellowship in Philippi.

These things took place many years ago. Our Philippian Christ-followers have increased in number, and I've become one of the leaders, one of Paul's co-workers along with Luke and others in this Roman colony city. We provided support for Paul and his co-workers while they were in Corinth because Paul wanted to avoid patronage from various locals who wanted him to be their in-house orator. Paul did not want to be a paid client in such a role. We, however, had a relationship built on giving and receiving. So, he was happy to have support from us while in Corinth.[2] We were eager as well to support the famine relief fund Paul was collecting in all the congregations he helped found for the Jerusalem church, which was suffering in various ways.

Most recently, we received a letter from Paul and found out he was under house arrest in Rome. The letter was warm and joyful despite this and honestly it made me weep. Paul seemed confident he would soon

---

1. See Acts 16:11–15.
2. On which see 2 Cor 8:1–4.

IN THE WORDS OF EUODIA

be released from this situation and be able to travel back east. Especially touching was the ending of his letter, where Paul said that we had done far more for him that he had asked and was gently saying let that be enough at this juncture. I hope he is right! If there really is a formal trial he will need a good lawyer who can speak Latin in court.[3]

I hear that Paul wants to return to Ephesos as Timothy needs some help from the "Apostle to the Gentiles," as he is now famously known. My hope is that he will come by way of the Roman road, the *Via Egnatia*, that stretches across Macedonia. Paul can then spend a few happy days with us as a free man. It is of course difficult to make Paul stay still, so fixed is he on accomplishing all that Christ wants him to do. Still, he has made clear how much he loves the followers of Christ in Philippi, so we may hope to see him again face to face.

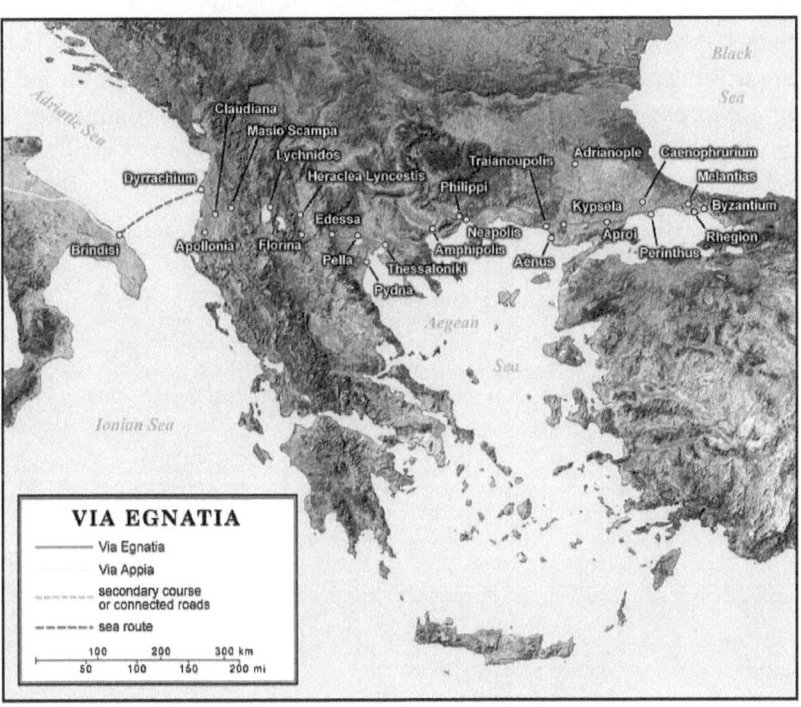

---

3. See the letter to the Philippians, particularly the first and last chapters. In fact, it is likely that Paul was released from house arrest in Rome because: 1) he was a Roman citizen, and 2) his Jewish opponents likely did not make the required trek to Rome to present their case, in which instance the charges would be dropped.

Meanwhile, maybe Luke can help me iron out some differences with Syntyche.[4] We frankly don't agree on how to expand our witness to some of the Romans who live here. The Romans have a long history of disliking the Jewish people. With the emperor cult rising in popularity, the civic pressure is increasing to do more to require everyone to participate in the public festivals in honor of Nero, which definitely have religious aspects. Syntyche doesn't really see the problem with participation since, as she frequently says quoting Paul "there is no god but one," so why not eat meat sacrificed in honor of the emperor at one of the temples? However, this will scandalize our more conservative Jewish followers of Jesus. Further, we don't want to draw any more public attention to the Jews under the present circumstances. Clement, who himself is a Roman citizen, thinks this matter must not be allowed to fester. It threatens to imperil all the progress we have made in the last several years here spreading the good news. It's a delicate matter. But now that Paul has insisted that Syntyche and I be of one mind, I'm trusting cooler heads will prevail when we go to the jailer's house for a prayer meeting. May the Lord himself watch over us in the coming weeks as we make some decisions.

---

4. See Phil 4:2.

IN THE WORDS OF SERGIUS PAULUS

Lucius Sergius Paulus was a Roman of note. He held several positions but the chronology remains subject to debate.[1] In the mid-40s AD, he was appointed by Emperor Claudius as a "curator" of the banks and channels of the Tiber River which flows through Rome. He may have spent a short time in this position but his name is etched in stone! We also find Sergius Paulus serving as a proconsul in the capital city of Paphos on the island of Cyprus (Kupros). Most believe this is the same man who met with Paul, Barnabas, and John Mark. Sergius Paulus was apparently converted to Christianity (Acts 13:6–12) and encouraged Paul to go to Pisidian Antioch, his home region. The below honorary inscription, with the name of Paulus, L. Sergius, was found in Pisidian Antioch.

Painting of Sergius Paulus sitting in his curule chair while Paul blinds Elymas, by Raphael

---

1. See Bryon Windle, "Sergius Paulus, an Archaeological Biography," *Bible Archaeology Report* (November 15, 2019).

I am Lucius Sergius Paulus, of Pisidian Antioch. My climb up the *cursus honorum,* the ladder of success, has been rapid. At present I am *consul suffectus.* Before that I was proconsul at Paphos in Kupros, and before that I was appointed curator of the banks and the river Tiber during the reign of Claudius. It went well enough that I was then dispatched by the Senate to Kupros. But my home region, where my relatives still live, is a town on the border of Pisidia and Galatia—Pisidian Antioch.

Like most Romans, since I respect and honor the gods, I consult them from time to time when a major decision must be made. And there are many such decisions when one is governing a place like Kupros, which is home to many Greeks, Jews, but not as many Romans. So, sometimes I also consult prophets and sages when some decision seems especially difficult.

I have always been curious about the soul and especially Elysium or the realm of the gods. The Jews have much to say about these matters, so occasionally I called on Bar-Jesus, who seems to be a genuine Jewish prophet of sorts. Among other things he seemed to be able to foresee the future, as well as consult the shades of the ancestors, including mine. Further, he had skill in reading the stars, the flight of birds, and the inner organs of animals. So, he had become a part of my entourage.

Then there came a day when other Jews showed up in my court claiming to have some "good news" for me and others. Unexpectedly, there was a confrontation between Bar-Jesus and these men, who accused him of being a false prophet trying to take advantage of my interest in the supernatural. They even called him a *magus,* the word for a charlatan or a sorcerer, and thus some sort of spiritual danger to me. The confrontation did not last long, but it resulted in a man who shared my Roman name, Paulus, saying to Bar-Jesus: "You are a child of the devil and an enemy of everything that is right! You are full of all kinds of deceit and trickery. Will you never stop perverting the right ways of the Lord? Now the hand of the Lord is against you. You are going to be blind for a time, not even able to see the light of the sun." And, sure enough, Bar-Jesus became blind instantly and had to be led away by the hand![2]

Clearly, this man Paulus had some god on his side, and so I was inclined to listen to him. The result was that I accepted this Jesus that Paulus was speaking about and rejected the Jesus that had been part of my court. I thanked Paulus for opening my eyes to the deceptions of that false prophet. In gratitude I wrote a letter of introduction for Paulus, and suggested he

2. See Acts 13:6–12.

IN THE WORDS OF SERGIUS PAULUS

go share his good news message in my home region, especially in Pisidian Antioch, my hometown. I am happy to say he and his companions traveled to Pisidian Antioch, no easy trek.

All that, however, was many years ago. I am now *consul suffectus* in Rome. As for the other Paulus, he died through the orders of the mad Nero who sought to blame Christ followers for the horrible fire that happened here six years ago. Confidentially, I am thankful Nero is no longer our emperor. Claudius had been a much better emperor before Nero, and we need somebody like him now. We have gone through three emperors in three years!

In the eastern part of the Empire, General Vespasian was proclaimed emperor by his troops after the quelling of the Jewish rebels, though his son Titus had to finish the job and besiege Jerusalem. Vespasian challenged Vitellius's army in northern Italy and won decisively. He has come to Rome, and already things have begun to settle down into the old patterns during Claudius's day. Vespasian is very much a traditional Roman with traditional values, which is more than can be said about his immediate predecessors. He is the one who recently reviewed my record and made me *consul suffectus*. I am grateful.

I note that Vespasian has installed a new Jewish prophet here in Rome, one Flavius Josephus, a former Jewish commander of some of the rebels. Apparently, he foretold that Vespasian would soon be emperor while he was still a general fighting in Judaea and Galilee. These are strange times.

I still have hope that the good news I heard on Kupros is indeed true. To that end, from time to time, I visit the catacombs where some Christ followers meet. I met a woman called Priscilla who worked with Paulus in Corinth and Ephesos. I accepted her invitation to come to their worship time. I have to admit it was uplifting, even joyful. I think I may have just found the spiritual food I've been longing for all my adult life. Time will tell.

At my age, with my wife long since passed away and my children grown up and scattered to the winds, some back to Pisidian Antioch, I could use some comfort and joy. But I am glad to have a more settled life in the Eternal City. I do not suppose I shall ever return to Pisidian Antioch, but I hear they have erected an honorific column for me there.

IN THE WORDS OF DEMETRIUS, THE SILVERSMITH—PAUL'S NEMESIS IN EPHESUS

Demetrius of Ephesus was apparently the leader of the Silversmiths Guild when Paul visited c. AD 51. He would have been a wealthy and influential man because many pilgrims came to Ephesus to worship the Greek goddess Artemis (aka the Roman goddess Diana). Like all tourists, they buy souvenirs, the most expensive being a solid silver likeness of Artemis herself or a mini-shrine for their homes. Or perhaps they would like a mini-replica of her magnificent temple. Today there is only really one column left of the Temple of Artemis, once one of the Seven Wonders of the Ancient World. In Acts 19, Paul tells the story of his near-death experience in Ephesus.

Photo of Ephesian Artemis, Ephesus Museum, Ann Witherington.

Sometimes it takes an ordinary person like me, a person with business sense, to see a danger to one's city. And Saul or Paul or whatever he called himself was definitely a danger. There are many Jews who live in my city of Ephesos but, generally speaking, they cause little trouble. They keep their ridiculous idea about there being only one god (theirs of course) to themselves. They don't go proclaiming this heresy all over the city. And non-Jews are not usually encouraged to follow their rituals or beliefs.

Paul however was different. He was spreading insane notions about a man named Jesus who got himself crucified by the Roman governor in Jerusalem. They claimed that he rose from the dead and later ascended up into the sky! And now they say he is a God with a capital G—the only GOD! This message was called εὐαγγελίον—good news! It's certainly not good news to any of us Greeks here in Ephesus. It reminds me of the propaganda from the emperors about the good news of taking over one country after another to build the Roman Empire!

Anyway, we Greeks don't believe in the Jewish notion that somebody could come back from the dead in a physical body. The body is the prison house of the soul. And furthermore, crucifixion is the most shameful way to die. No one comes back from that condemnation with an honorable standing in society. To the contrary, we would say that person was condemned or cursed by the gods to that horrible fate. And yet amazingly people actually believe this nonsense.

Now for the bad news. This preaching about Jesus being not only the Jewish Messiah but also a savior for all Gentiles was negatively affecting my business. I sell silver shrines for your home worship, and little silver replicas of the great statue of Artemis, the goddess who blesses our city with fruitfulness and prosperity, and little replicas of her magnificent temple as well. These are mementos that the pilgrims to Ephesos can take home, and indeed use as reminders to pray to and thank the goddess Artemis for their fertile crops or offspring or prosperity in general. My business was dwindling because of this Paulos and his incessant proclamation in the markets, in the hall of Tyrannus, and on the street corners.

One day, I could take it no longer. I went around explaining to my fellow merchants and citizens what a danger this was to our life and livelihood. Finally, when this did not galvanize everyone, I called a meeting of the guild of craftsmen and said words to the following effect:

> You know, my friends, that we receive a good income from this business. And you see and hear how this fellow Paul has convinced and led astray large numbers of people here in Ephesos and in practically the whole province of Asia. He says that gods made by human hands are no gods at all. There is danger that our trade will lose its good name. There is danger also that the temple of the great goddess Artemis will be discredited. And, worst of all, there is danger that the goddess herself, who is worshiped throughout

the province of Asia and the world, will be robbed of her divine majesty.[1]

Finally, the danger registered with my fellow craftsmen. They became enraged and began shouting, "Great is Artemis of the Ephesians!" They went out in the streets and kept chanting. Soon much of the city was joining them as well. I thought, at last we will drive these Jesus people out of the city. Things got a bit chaotic and two of Paulos's Macedonian co-workers, Gaius and Aristarchus, were seized and dragged into the great theater. I found out later that Paulos was planning on addressing the crowd in the theater, but some of the city officials he had befriended dissuaded him from this, and he was hustled out of town.

As so often happens, many people seeing the crowd going to the theater didn't know what it was really all about, and there was confusion coupled with curiosity. Then suddenly, the city clerk showed up. He quieted the crowd down and explained that if anyone had a legal case, and he mentioned me by name, against Gaius and Aristarchus, the place for that to be dealt with was the court of law, what we call the basilica. I was not interested in Gaius and Aristarchus. I knew the real instigator was Paulos, but he had been hustled out of town by the time the meeting in the theater was finished and the crowd dispersed.

In due course the clerk got credit for quelling a potential riot. He claimed that the Macedonians had not blasphemed Artemis or attempted to plunder or desecrate the temple. So, they were allowed to stay in Ephesos and no action was taken against Paulos. I was disgusted, but there was nothing I could do about it. After all, Ephesos was a city of many gods and, while one philosopher said that Olympus is overcrowded, most people think that honoring one more so-called god like Jesus the Christ or anointed one can do no harm, even if it does no good. But I will be on the lookout in case Paul returns. He's dangerous!

---

1. Acts 19:26–28.

IN THE WORDS OF DEMETRIUS

The Theater of Ephesus

Archaeologists say you can judge the size of the city by multiplying by ten from the capacity of its theater. If so, when this theater was built in the 3rd century BC there were already about 150,000 people living in Ephesus. By Paul's day, the highest estimates suggest over 250,000, but this is disputed due to the geography of the area. Regardless, Ephesus was the third largest city in the Mediterranean world, after Rome and Alexandria.

IN THE WORDS OF TITUS—PAUL'S "TRUE SON"

Titus is never mentioned in the Acts of the Apostles. But he was certainly an early Christian missionary, a well-educated, uncircumcised Greek Gentile converted by Paul himself. In the Letter to Titus (1:4), Paul refers to him as "my true son in our common faith." We hear about Titus in Galatians 2:1, 3 because in AD 49 he went with Paul and Barnabas to Jerusalem for the famous Council. We also have records of Titus being in Ephesus (Turkey), Nicopolis (Western Greece), and in Corinth (Southern Greece), where he brought a letter from Paul asking for money for the poor in Jerusalem, and in Dalmatia (now Croatia). Titus was in Philippi, Macedonia with Paul and helped him to write 2 Corinthians, which Titus personally delivered to the disciples in Corinth. Eventually he settled on the island of Crete, which many consider his home. Eusebius wrote in his *Ecclesiastical History* that Titus became the first bishop of Crete and that he was buried there. Interestingly, the Epistle to Titus is addressed to him and describes the duties of elders and bishops.

Image of Titus from the ruins of Church of Titus on the south side of the island of Crete.

Somehow, I am not mentioned in Luke's chronicle of the spread of the good news from Jerusalem all the way to Rome. Never mind, there are many others not mentioned by him as well, such as Andronicus and Junia. I am a Greek. My friend and mentor, Paul, referred to me as "my true son

IN THE WORDS OF TITUS—PAUL'S "TRUE SON"

in the common faith." In truth he was indeed like a father to both me and Timothy.

I was one of the first non-Jewish converts to the following of Christ. This is surely why Paul took me with him to Jerusalem, as a proof that non-Jews could become followers of Christ without first becoming Jews. That early meeting in Jerusalem with the so-called "pillars" of the new movement was contentious but, at the same time, positive, because they agreed that Paul should go to the Gentiles and Simon Peter to the Jews outside of Judaea. The end result of this decision still left many questions unanswered because, though no requirement of circumcision was imposed on me, there were some insisting I must "Judaize" in order to be a full-fledged follower of Christ. Fortunately, Paul stood firm on that issue. He wanted some co-workers to remain non-Jews so they could more easily reach out to other Greeks and Romans. After all, there was considerable prejudice against the Jews especially because of their belief that there is only one God.

The decisive meeting in Jerusalem was exactly at the midway point of this century and all the principal leaders were there. After Peter went off to Bithynia and elsewhere, the leadership of the Jerusalem community fell on the shoulders of Jesus' brother Jacob. He had gained the name of Jacob the Just, as he continued to remain true to Torah and was respected even by many Jews who were not Christ followers. This meeting would prove to be a real turning point in our movement, not least because both Jacob and Peter agreed that Gentiles did not need to become Jews to be full-fledged members of the body of Christ. Yes, there were some Pharisaic Christ followers there who insisted that the Gentiles be circumcised and forced to keep the Mosaic law.

Somewhat surprisingly, in light of his behavior in Antioch earlier, it was Peter who stood up and said no. Peter had seen the fruit of Paul of the missions led by Paul and his co-workers. Peter was able to say:

> Brothers, you know that some time ago God made a choice among you that the Gentiles might hear from my lips the message of the gospel and believe. God, who knows the heart, showed that he accepted them by giving the Holy Spirit to them, just as he did to us. He did not discriminate between us and them, for he purified their hearts by faith. Now then, why do you try to test God by putting on the necks of Gentiles a yoke that neither we nor our ancestors have been able to bear? No! We believe it is through the grace of our Lord Jesus that we are saved, just as they are.[2]

2. Acts 15:7–11.

Then Paul and Barnabas testified about the success of their work and even the miracles that sometimes accompanied it. And the whole meeting became silent, awaiting the reaction of Jacob as the one who could now speak for the Jerusalem church.

In the end, Jacob found a compromise he believed was Spirit-led and approved by the elders with him. It involved only that the Gentiles honor the heart of the Mosaic law, namely, that there be no more idolatry and immorality. In particular they must stay away from pagan feasts at pagan temples. Why? These feasts involved the worship of false gods, the consumption of meat sacrificed to those so-called gods, the consumption of blood and things strangled, sexual misbehavior and orgies—in short, all things abhorrent to Jews and new Christians! Paul was very pleased with this limited restriction. Silas was commissioned to travel with him and read out the decree of Jacob about these things. With the agreement of Jacob, Peter, and Paul on these matters, the matter was largely settled, apart from some rear-guard actions by some disgruntled Pharisaic Jewish followers of Jesus. But the future of the movement did not lie in their hands.

I only became a full co-worker of Paul during the second missionary journey through Galatia and on to Troas and then Macedonia and Greece. I spent considerable time as the emissary of Paul in Corinth when he couldn't be there. There were many divisions in that group of house churches and there was the further problem of some false teachers filling their heads with criticisms of Paul and his ministry. The Corinthians had not responded well to a stern letter Paul wrote to them. I was sent to find out what was happening there. I was able to bring back a report to Paul in Philippi that the stern letter actually had a good effect in the end. The troublemakers had either gone quiet or repentant! In any case, things were better than when Paul wrote them.[3] I was, in fact, the one who delivered and read Paul's fourth letter to the Corinthians at various household meetings there.[4] It helped heal some of the rifts.

I was further tasked with the job of soliciting money from Corinth to be a love offering for the poor and needy in the Jerusalem assembly. They were undergoing a rather severe famine and, as Christ followers, they had been cut off from the regular dole to widows and orphans in Jerusalem sponsored by the Jewish authorities.

---

3. On all this see 2 Cor 8:6–16.

4. This is the letter we call 2 Corinthians, but it was preceded by one referred to in 1 Corinthians 5, then 1 Corinthians, then the severe letter, then 2 Corinthians.

IN THE WORDS OF TITUS—PAUL'S "TRUE SON"

Much later Paul sent me to establish the first Christ follower groups on my home island of Crete. He wrote me a detailed letter on how to go about appointing elders in each town or village. I was there for many years until Paul sent Artemis and Tychicus to relieve me for a while, so that I could meet him in Nicopolis in western Greece (Titus 3:12). At the very end of Paul's life, I was with him in Rome and he sent me to Dalmatia to do more evangelizing (2 Tim 4:10). Eventually being Bishop of Crete was a highlight of my long, fulfilling career.

When I am asked what sort of person Paul was, I say he was "inspired and inspiring"! Being inspired, he was driven, a man with a sense of urgency about the work of God that he was doing. He realized that his life could easily come to a sudden halt. There was so much opposition to him and his proclamation of the good news in various places including in synagogues in the diaspora.

When you saw his dedication and courage, it was contagious. He inspired you to help him, please him and so please God. When I read out the letter I took to Corinth and got to the portion about his hardships, I choked up. The tears just flowed down my cheeks as I read,

> I have worked much harder, been in prison more frequently, been flogged more severely, and been exposed to death again and again. Five times I received from the Jews the forty lashes minus one. Three times I was beaten with rods, once I was pelted with stones, three times I was shipwrecked, I spent a night and a day in the open sea, I have been constantly on the move. I have been in danger from rivers, in danger from bandits, in danger from my fellow Jews, in danger from Gentiles; in danger in the city, in danger in the country, in danger at sea; and in danger from false believers. I have labored and toiled and have often gone without sleep; I have known hunger and thirst and have often gone without food; I have been cold and naked. Besides everything else, I face daily the pressure of my concern for all the churches. Who is weak, and I do not feel weak? Who is led into sin, and I do not inwardly burn?[5]

One has to admit, this is an odd thing to boast about but, as Paul said, God's power is most evident in our weaknesses. When people see our weaknesses and yet the power of God working through us, it becomes evident that the mere mortal is not the source this power, God is. I miss those days of hearing Paul proclaim the God-whispered words of the gospel. But the good news work continues and is never done!

---

5. 2 Cor 11:23–29.

IN THE WORDS OF CRISPUS, THE SYNAGOGUE LEADER—PAUL'S CONVERT IN CORINTH

Crispus originally came from Chalcedon, a town in the region of Bithynia on the coast of the Black Sea. Today it is a suburb of Istanbul. According to Acts 18:8 he was the chief of the synagogue at Corinth. Thus, he was a learned Jew. Crispus and his whole family were converted by Paul as recorded in Acts 18:8 and 1 Corinthians 1:14. He is traditionally listed among the seventy disciples recorded in Luke 10:1. According to tradition he later served as bishop of Chalcedon and was martyred for his new faith in Jesus as the Messiah.

This lintel was found in old Corinth. It says "synagogue of Hebrews" but a synagogue has not yet been found in Corinth.

Stained glass window of Paul baptizing a convert (Crispus?). Location unknown.

IN THE WORDS OF CRISPUS

Sometimes I ask myself, what has happened to me since I met Paul? I was doing quite well in Corinth as the new leader in the synagogue of the Hebrews. Paul came to town with quite a pedigree—trained in Jerusalem under Gamaliel, a Hebrew of Hebrews, a zealous Jew who knew the Scriptures very well. He seemed like a fine candidate to preach in our synagogue. So, what harm could it do to let this learned man speak? Little did I know what would happen when he opened his mouth to open God's Word. Suddenly we were hearing about how our long hoped-for Messiah already came; how he died for our sins, making other sacrifices for sins unnecessary; how God vindicated him beyond death by raising him; and how he appeared to many Jews, including Paul himself. The thing about this incredible testimony was that it seemed to be both the fulfillment of our deepest hopes but too incredible to be true. And yet something happened when I heard this testimony. I found myself filled with God's Spirit, who whispered in my heart, "It's true, embrace it."

The next thing I knew, Paul asked me if I believed what he said. I found myself saying yes! My wife also had tears in her eyes and the children were jumping with joy. Before I knew it Paul was leading us to water where we were all baptized. It happened all in one day! I woke up the next morning wondering if it was all a dream.[1]

There are still days when I ask myself, have I just ruined our lives? We are now shunned by our fellow Jews in Corinth, even close friends and relatives. But now we have new friends! Paul and Priscilla and Aquila have been quick to fill the void. Paul's rhetoric is powerful and persuasive. He's unlike so many orators who come and go, or charlatans trying to sell you something. Paul genuinely cares about us and reassures us that God does as well. And he demonstrates this time and again when things get rough. We have meals together and talk through our troubles. Paul puts things in a broader perspective. One day he was praying for us and saying,

> Praise be to the God and Father of our Lord Jesus Christ, the Father of compassion and the God of all comfort, who comforts us in all our troubles, so that we can comfort those in any trouble with the comfort we ourselves receive from God. For just as we share abundantly in the sufferings of Christ, so also our comfort abounds through Christ. If we are distressed, it is for your comfort and salvation; if we are comforted, it is for your comfort, which produces in you patient endurance of the same sufferings we

---

1. Cf. Acts 18:8 and 1 Cor 1:14.

suffer. And our hope for you is firm because we know that just as you share in our sufferings, so also you share in our comfort.[2]

My wife has been nervous about the long-term impact of this major change in our lives, but so far we have managed to keep our family wine business profitable. Paul has now moved to stay with Phoebe in Cenchreae, so we see less of him except when he is working in the leatherworkers shop just off the Lechaion Road. He's been here for over a year and the number of new followers of Christ keeps climbing. I just hope there is no further trouble, but I hear rumors that some of my fellow Jews are thinking of taking Paul to court. That is unlikely to end well, but for now all is quiet.

Paul wrote to my fellow Corinthians recently to warn about the problems of having the church divided over the issue of who is leading. I'll quote him for you. He even mentions me by name. I certainly remember the day he baptized me!

> I appeal to you, brothers and sisters, in the name of our Lord Jesus Christ, that all of you agree with one another in what you say and that there be no divisions among you, but that you be perfectly united in mind and thought. My brothers and sisters, some from Chloe's household have informed me that there are quarrels among you. What I mean is this: One of you says, "I follow Paul"; another, "I follow Apollos"; another, "I follow Cephas"; still another, "I follow Christ." Is Christ divided? Was Paul crucified for you? Were you baptized in the name of Paul? I thank God that I did not baptize any of you except Crispus and Gaius, so no one can say that you were baptized in my name. (Yes, I also baptized the household of Stephanas; beyond that, I don't remember if I baptized anyone else.) For Christ did not send me to baptize but to preach the gospel—not with wisdom and eloquence, lest the cross of Christ be emptied of its power.[3]

It is hard to know how long things will stay quiet here in Corinth. Recently, Erastus the aedile has become a Christ follower here, and this has caused an enormous stir among the Romans in town. The latest is he has invited us to meet in his villa on the edge of town, which is a much larger venue than any of the existing houses where we meet. Sometimes I ask the Lord, what's next? The prospects are both exciting and frightening at the same time. But I and my family have learned to leave the future in God's hands, and live with anticipation and the knowledge that God is not finished with us yet.

2. 2 Cor 1:3–7.
3. 1 Cor 1:10–17.

IN THE WORDS OF GALLIO—PAUL'S JUDGE IN CORINTH

Gallio (originally Lucius Annaeanus Novatus) was born in Cordoba, Spain in 5 BC. His father was Seneca the Elder and his brother was the more famous writer Seneca the Younger. For some reason he was adopted by Lucius Junius Gallio, a well-known rhetorician. Thus, his new and formal name became Lucius Junius Gallio Annaeanus. Apparently, he and his brother went to Rome when Seneca was asked to tutor the young Nero. Gallio rose up in the Roman ranks to become, in the words of Emperor Claudius, "my friend and proconsul," serving in Corinth in AD 51–52. Thus, we can say that Paul was definitely in Corinth at this same time. In Acts 18:12–17 we read that Paul was brought to Gallio's *bema*, the judgment seat, by Sosthenes, the head of the local synagogue. The charges were typical: Paul was accused of violating the Roman law of religious tolerance by claiming Jesus was the one and only true God and the true Messiah of the Hebrews. Gallio dismissed the charges and had all the Jewish rabble-rousers removed from his court.

This honorific inscription was found at Delphi and records the words of Claudius: "Gallio, my friend and proconsul."

It not only dates Gallio's time in Corinth to AD 51–52 but also helps us plot the time line of Paul's ministry.

ENCOUNTERS WITH PAUL

I am Lucius Junius Gallio Annaeanus. I was adopted by the man who bears the same three first names, a famous rhetorician. My older brother, Seneca, is the well-known Stoic philosopher. My brother and I were banished to Corsica for a while (long story!) but recalled in AD 48 when Agrippina the Younger wanted Seneca to be the tutor for her son Nero.

I was a senator rising up the *cursus honorum*[1] and was assigned as proconsul to the newly created province of Achaea. Corinth was named the capital in a deliberate snub to Athens! It was my friend Claudius who saw that I got this new posting towards the end of his reign, before he was poisoned. Unfortunately for me, the atmosphere in and around Corinth did not promote good health nor did the physicians I saw! This affected my disposition and ability to administer a full term as proconsul. I returned to Rome after a couple of years in Corinth.

Nero came to Corinth while I was there and it was my duty to entertain him. Much later he came back and, having changed the rules of the games to include the arts along with sports, he competed in the poetry and lyre-playing contests. Naturally, he won the poetry and lyre contests! Need I say more. He had changed the rules for all the Olympic-style games to make it possible for him to show off. Since he's still emperor now, please don't mention this in public.

The general drudgery of being a proconsul in a Roman province among other things involved sitting on the *bema* in Corinth and judging boring cases of theft, bribery, and so on. But on one occasion a case was brought against a tentmaker named Saul of Tarsus (he usually goes by Paul now). The man was a Roman citizen, rather well known in the city. He had made friends with the recently elected aedile Erastus, whom I conferred with before the trial. Actually, there wasn't a proper trial. When it became apparent that this was a squabble between Jews about purely religious matters pertaining to Judaism, I threw the case out of court. Surprisingly, the synagogue leader who had brought the case to trial was beaten right in front of me by his own people! In any case, I would have exonerated Paul as a Roman citizen, for Roman law always protects its own. Like Paul, I became a Roman citizen in a foreign land, so I can relate!

Soon after this incident, I left to return to Rome, where things went from bad to worse. First there was the great fire that burned down whole regions of Rome. Rumor had it that Nero wanted this to happen so he could

---

1. The *cursus honorum* is what we would call the corporate ladder of success, but in this case it has to do with increasing honor as well as position.

IN THE WORDS OF GALLIO—PAUL'S JUDGE IN CORINTH

rebuild that part of the city according to his own grandiose design. Then there was a plan to assassinate Nero not long thereafter. While my brother was not involved, he was accused and took his own life. Now they are attacking me in the Senate. I fear I must follow the same course as Seneca.

The first five years of Nero's reign were a golden age of peace and prosperity. In those days, Seneca and Afranius Burrus, the prefect of the Praetorian Guard, were running the ship of state while Nero went to and acted in plays and contests, fancying himself an artist! Ha! He had neither the dignity, nor the work ethic, nor the integrity of my brother and myself. Even Paul the Jew was a better and more moral human being providing good service to the city he lived in. I think I shall reprise on my mausoleum the famous Epicurean dictum, "*Non fui, fui, non sum, non curo.*"—"I was not, I was, I am not, I care not!"

This bema is a raised rostrum in the middle of Corinth's Roman forum. Here the city officials spoke to the people and pronounced judgments.

A curule chair on which the proconsul would sit on top of the bema to pronounce judgment.

IN THE WORDS OF APOLLOS—
PAUL'S COLLEAGUE IN EPHESUS AND CORINTH

Apollos came from Alexandria. He is first mentioned preaching in Ephesus around AD 52–53. However, after meeting Priscilla and Aquila, he learned much more about the new faith. For starters, he had only known about John's baptism. Now it was time to learn about the new baptism in Jesus. It was Priscilla and Aquila who took Apollos under their wing and "explained to him the way of God more adequately" (Acts 18:26). Apollos next went to Corinth, the provincial capital of Achaia. He arrived there with a letter of recommendation from the Christians living in Ephesus. Apparently, the Ephesians were pleased with Apollos because they wrote that he "greatly helped those who through grace had believed, for he powerfully refuted the Jews in public, showing by the Scriptures that the Christ was Jesus" (Acts 18:27–28). When Paul wrote to the Corinthians (c. AD 55), he mentioned Apollos saying, "I planted, Apollos watered, but God gave the growth" (1 Cor 3:6).

Icon of Apollos from the icon shop in Meteora.

According to tradition, Apollos served as bishop of Crete later in his life. Some scholars believe that he was also Bishop of Corinth, then Smyrna in Turkey, and finally the port city of Caesarea in Judaea. Many scholars believe he wrote the Epistle to the Hebrews.

IN THE WORDS OF APOLLOS

Fresco of Sosthenes, Apollo, Cephas, Tychicus, Epaphroditus,
Cæsar and Onesiphorus from the Menologion of Basil II

Sometimes the stories one hears about a person in advance of meeting them grossly exaggerate the reality of who that person is and what he has done. In the case of Paul, the Apostle to the Gentiles, the stories hardly did him justice. His larger-than-life image in the tales I heard hardly scratched the surface of his real nature and accomplishments. He was not merely a trailblazer for a new religious movement within Judaism, he was an agent of dramatic change in some cases.

I first encountered his co-workers, Priscilla and Aquila, in Ephesos when I was traveling around sharing the good news about Jesus. You may well ask how a person like me, from Alexandria in Egypt, came to be a follower of Jesus of Nazareth. The answer is not complicated.

As a Jew, I regularly went up to the festivals in Jerusalem, and on various occasions heard Jesus' teaching in the temple precincts and elsewhere. As someone who was raised in an educated and socially elite family, I knew the Hebrew Scriptures in their Greek translation, for Egypt is where that translation was made. I was always wondering when and where the Jewish messiah would come to help our people, and I had especially studied the later prophets Isaiah and Daniel and also the Psalms to try to understand what was to come.

I must admit that I got overly excited as a young man when Jesus rode into Jerusalem on a donkey and people were chanting the line from the Psalms, "blessed is he who comes in the name of the Lord." I was confused initially by Jesus' actions in the temple during that last week, but then I remembered that the Essenes had also warned about the corruption in the temple, not least the corruption of requiring Jews to exchange Jewish coins for the pagan Tyrian shekel with images of demigods and eagles on it to pay the temple tax. This was shocking, and Jesus was right to object. I was even there on the Mount of Olives when Jesus warned that the temple would be judged, desecrated by the Romans within a generation. Nonetheless, I was completely shocked by the crucifixion of Jesus. Jews did not expect a crucified messiah. No one read even Isaiah's servant songs that way. That seemed to be the tragic end of a remarkable ministry, that is, until Jesus began to appear to various of his disciples and others.

I had lingered in Jerusalem after Jesus' death to see what might happen next. After all, I was there to celebrate Passover and Jesus died on the eve of the festival. I was also present when Jesus appeared to more than five hundred people at one time. Remember that we were not visionaries! We did not see him in heaven; we saw him on earth! We talked and broke bread with him until he literally vanished! I did not go up to Galilee but heard there were more appearances there.

All of this left me with much to ponder. I went back to Alexandria to search the Scriptures. It dawned on me, based on what I had heard Jesus say at his last Passover meal with the Twelve, that Jesus saw his death as the final necessary atoning sacrifice for sins, the death that made all other literal sacrifices both unnecessary and pointless. This in turn meant that we no longer needed a priesthood of the traditional sort or, for that matter, a temple where such sacrifices would be offered. Eventually I would work all these thoughts out in a sermon I wrote for the Hebrews in Rome, many years later. Jesus had indeed inaugurated a better, indeed a new covenant that eclipsed all previous ones.

Of course, in the early days there were gaps in my knowledge. I did not know that Jesus had also inaugurated a new covenant sign, namely baptism, when he was in Galilee. Now Jesus himself never baptized anyone. In fact, he himself was baptized by John in the Jordan. For a long time after Jesus' death and resurrection, John's baptism was the only sort I knew anything about. At first, I assumed that Jesus simply decided to continue John's practice. I was wrong about that.

IN THE WORDS OF APOLLOS

And so it was that in the early 50s I met Priscilla and Aquila in Ephesos. They heard me teaching and exhorting in the synagogue there. After the service they took me aside and explained to me more accurately the view of baptism that Jesus had instituted. It was not a baptism of repentance like John's, meant only for adults. It was not like the sign of the Mosaic covenant, that is, circumcision, only practiced on men. No, it was a covenant sign for men and women alike indicating that by God's grace the baptized were included in the new covenant community. In other words, it was a symbol of God's grace, which comes before and enables our response to the gift of salvation. As such, this led to the baptism of whole families, whole households—men, women, children, and even infants. God's salvation was for all persons of whatever age and stage of life.

Once Priscilla and Aquila had straightened me out about this in Ephesos, I requested a letter of introduction from them to go and spend time with the house church meetings in Corinth. When I got there, I tried to make clear that I was there to supplement and support Paul's work, not supplant it. As Paul later put it, he planted and I watered the plant, and it was all part of one gospel effort. Unfortunately, the Corinthians had other ideas, based in part on who baptized whom. I noticed some boasting "I am of Paul" and others "I am of Apollos." I tried to explain that the grace of God came to them not from the human agent, but from God, while we were just the human servants of Christ and his work. Apparently, some Corinthians had some magical ideas about religious rituals, which had to be corrected again and again. I imagine this is because of the secret initiation rites in the mystery cults.

The Villa of the Mysteries in Pompeii, Italy features a dining room decorated with frescoes dating to 70–60 BC, which probably depict the initiation of a woman into the Mystery Cult of Dionysius.

I later learned that the Corinthians, after Paul had baptized some of them, had actually practiced proxy baptism on behalf of their dead loved ones, hoping that would benefit them in the afterlife. Paul explained such practices were futile, especially if they did not believe in the Christian final form of the afterlife—resurrection.

After my initial time in Ephesos and Corinth, I went on to Philippi where I heard that Paul had been arrested in Jerusalem. This was troubling news, but I knew the Apostle to the Gentiles would say that God would use this for the advancement of the gospel. It was some four years later that Paul appealed to Caesar and was finally freed from house arrest in Caesarea.

I returned to Ephesos because that city was such fertile soil for the gospel and the Ephesians were enamored with rhetoric. I had skills in that area to use for the Lord. Timothy had been taken captive while I was there and I was hoping for his release so that we could both go to Rome and support the Christians there. One of the benefits of being in Ephesos is that copies of various of Paul's letters were there for me to read, including his letter to the Galatians and those sent to Corinth.[1]

The fire in Rome caused havoc in the Christ-follower household religious assemblies. I became concerned about reports that Jewish followers of Christ, who were being blamed for the fire, would retreat back into Judaism, a legal religion, renouncing their faith in Christ. They were certainly under pressure to do so. So, I was compelled to write my sermon for the Hebrews in Rome. I planned to follow it up with a visit, hopefully

---

1. On which see my, "The Influence of Galatians on Hebrews," *NTS* 37 (1991) 146–52. Note that in 2 Tim 4:13 Timothy is exhorted to come to Rome with the parchments that presumably had Paul's letters on them.

accompanied by Timothy. By the time we actually got there, Paul had been arrested again; Nero was blaming Christ followers for the fire; Paul was on the verge of being beheaded; and they were looking for Peter as well! These were dark days, to say the least.

In my sermon, I emphasized again and again that any sort of retrograde movement by Jewish followers of Christ would amount to apostasy from messianic Judaism. This was unacceptable! I strove to show how the new covenant was far superior to the old covenants. Only the new covenant provided full and complete salvation for God's people. I also stressed that Jesus the Messiah was the very wisdom of God, the very image of God come in the flesh, the full and final stage of God's revelation to us all. He is higher than the angels! Jesus made purification for sins, making unnecessary the earlier rites of atonement. Indeed, I stressed he is our high priest in heaven interceding for us with God the Father. Rather than turning back to Sinai, we need to press forward to the final revelation, the final theophany when Christ returns to Mount Zion and raises the dead. It is true that I have some emphases in that sermon that go beyond Paul's own major points, but I believe they don't go against them. For example, my emphasis on Christ as our heavenly high priest is not something Paul focused on in his letters.

When I got to Rome, it appeared that my sermon had been read out in various meetings with some beneficial effect. And now, I must continue the ministry of Paul with Jews and Gentiles as we face an uncertain future, already involving pressure, persecution, and even some executions. My benedictory word in that sermon can be applied to me and my situation as well as a prayer.

> Now may the God of peace, who through the blood of the eternal covenant brought back from the dead our Lord Jesus, that great Shepherd of the sheep, equip you with everything good for doing his will, and may he work in us what is pleasing to him, through Jesus Christ, to whom be glory for ever and ever. Amen.[2]

---

2. Heb 13:20–21.

IN THE WORDS OF PRISCILLA—
PAUL'S MOST FAMOUS FEMALE CO-WORKER

Priscilla (formally Prisca) and her husband Aquila were of Jewish heritage, probably from Pontus, a region on the southern coast of the Black Sea, who settled in Rome. They were tentmakers like Paul. Expelled from Rome thanks to the Emperor Claudius, they went to Corinth c. AD 49–50, where they met and worked with Paul (Acts 18:2–3; 18:18). Given that they seemed deeply knowledgeable about the Way, they were probably Christians before they met Paul. From Corinth they sailed away with Paul to Syria (Acts 18:8). The couple eventually returned to Rome c. 58 and then traveled to Ephesus. In 2 Timothy 4:19 we read that Paul asked Timothy, then working in Ephesus, to greet Priscilla and Aquila. Note that Priscilla seems quite comfortable sharing the gospel and instructing Apollos (Acts 18:26). As a friend and co-worker of Paul, she is considered an example of a female preacher and teacher and missionary. Paul certainly complimented the couple on a number of occasions (Rom 16:3; 1 Cor 16:19; 2 Tim 4:19). In all, there are six references to this dynamic couple.

Paracletos Greek Orthodox Monastery
Anderson, South Carolina.
http://www.greekorthodoxmonastery.org.

It seems so very long ago and worlds away. Aquila and I were working away in our leatherworking shop, minding our own business, when along came a bearded man named Saul, with a Greek name of Paul, asking if we could use any help. Normally, people came to us for any and all kinds of leather items—wineskins, satchels, tents, sandals, even garments of a sort. Not this earnest man! He saw that we were leatherworkers, which was his trade as well in Tarsus, his hometown. Actually, we could use the help because the Isthmian games would be coming soon to Corinth. We had too many orders for small tents.

Like us, Paul was a Jew, so there was a natural kinship. Little did we know that, instead of him working for us, in the long run we would be his co-workers in Corinth, Ephesos, and Rome. Through a singular providence of our God, we discovered that Paul also had embraced Jesus as the Christ. Clearly, he was meant to find us here, after we had been expelled from Rome by Claudius due to arguments in the synagogues about Jesus.[1] The Romans in general do not much like those of us who are Jews. Partly this is because we refuse to participate in their religious festivals and worship the false gods, but it is also because of our distinctive practices like circumcision, abstaining from certain kinds of food, and avoiding normal work on the sabbath. They call us *atheoi*, without the gods, because we only believe in one God, the God of the Scriptures.[2] So we have become the butt of so many jokes, and satirical remarks by their writers, Horace and especially Juvenal. The animus has only gotten worse since the fire in Rome during Nero's reign. But I digress.

What was the Apostle to the Gentiles like, you ask? To be honest, he was exhausting. He was a force of nature with such conviction about the truth and his mission that it was contagious. Being used to the environment of skepticism and irony in Rome, with even writers like Cicero suggesting a certain ambivalence about whether the gods actually cared about human beings, it was refreshing to meet someone with such assurance about Torah and God's work among Jews and non-Jews alike. Aquila and I were quickly swept up in this enthusiasm for the Christ-follower movement. But we had eighteen months to work with Paul in Corinth and to see how things would go before committing ourselves to become traveling proselytizers.

Of course, when you are dealing with such a strong personality as Paul, there was seldom anyone who could be indifferent to his presence and

---

1. See Acts 18:1–4.

2. Ironically, *atheos* is the word from which we get "atheist," which, in the modern context, means without belief in any god. This was not the meaning of the word in the first century.

proclamation. Either you embraced it or you reacted in a strongly negative way. The synagogue rulers went both ways. Stephanos was converted but the other synagogue leader took Paul to court, where he lost, not least because Paul was a Roman citizen and Gallio saw this as a religious squabble between Jews. He was not wrong about that.

As for me, I admired Paul's unending bravery for the good news cause. He endured stoning, the thirty-nine lashes, and being beaten with Roman rods by mistake, for that should never have happened to a Roman citizen. And what incredible courage it took to demand an apology from those Philippian rulers who were hardened old military men mustered out from the Roman army. And then there was the riot in the theater in Ephesos. We had to get Paul out of town quickly after he had been there more than two years. He was protesting the whole way when we forced him to leave. Ephesos was not a Roman colony city, but still very much a Greek city, and he had little or no clout with the officials there. He couldn't assert his Roman citizenship and expect the officials to back off, especially since he was threatening the economic well-being of the city's shrine salesmen, who sold small statues of Artemis and her great temple.

It's been almost a decade since Paul went to be with the Lord, but his words and deeds are vivid in my mind. I am so glad that Luke is writing down Paul's story. Luke has returned to his home in Philippi these last decades since the death of the apostle and has acquired a patron named Theophilus. Luke has much to tell especially in regard to that third major missionary journey. There was the house arrest in Caesarea Maritima and again in Rome until finally Paul was freed for a short time. Luke's Greek is much better than mine! Some say he writes with eloquence. But then physicians have always been some of the most literate among us.

Our movement has continued to gain followers despite considerable opposition. Fortunately, the persecutions and prosecutions have been sporadic depending on the particular emperor in power. The Flavians, Vespasian and his sons, seem far more sensible than the mercurial Nero, and far more sane than mad Caligula or Claudius the Roman traditionalist. On the other hand, Titus, Vespasian's eldest, is the one who sacked the holy city of Jerusalem with hardly anything of consequence left of the temple and treasuries. I was there to see Titus's triumph with the parade of items stolen from the temple. Now they are building an arch to celebrate that triumph and Titus is promising to build a huge colosseum right beside it!

IN THE WORDS OF PRISCILLA

The arch of Titus, celebrating his triumph bringing back to Rome treasures from the Jerusalem temple which he pillaged after taking the city in A.D. 70.

As for me, I'm an old lady now, and am perceived to be no threat to anyone! I must say that's something of a relief. No one harasses me like in the old days of Claudius when I set out on the first day of the week to go to the catacombs for worship and meetings. People think it's perfectly natural for there to be rituals in such a place and honoring of the dead, in this case both Peter and Paul. I did notice, however, a new graffito in the entrance way to the catacomb in Rome. Someone drew a picture mocking a man named Alexamenos worshipping his God. The insult, however, was that the figure on the cross had a donkey head. Such a sad parody of what really happened when our Savior died for us all, indeed for the sins of the world. But still, it means the word about the crucified savior has gotten out, even to the most skeptical. The God-whispered words, once spoken, cannot be forever silenced, and they will produce reactions both positive and negative.[3]

3. The Alexamenos graffito from a catacomb reads, "Alexamenos worships his God."

The Alexamenos graffito was scratched into the wall of a room (catacomb?) on Palatine Hill in Rome. It had been dated to c. AD 100–200.

I suppose in some ways it is a good thing that our faith is not that of the rulers. They would co-opt it for their own purposes and, while life would become less of a challenge, at the same time if our faith became publicly acceptable and even popular, that might not be entirely a good thing. By this I mean that no one today is a *christianoi*, a partisan of Christ, because it is socially advantageous. There are no nominal followers of Christ. We are committed come what may and do what the authorities will do. It was no mere metaphor when Jesus said, "Take up your cross and follow me" or "He who would seek to save his life will lose it." The cost of discipleship is high.

We have just lit the lamps in the house. It is the season of the dying of the light so I must set aside my reverie and help prepare the meal. I will say this in closing. Other than Jesus, whom I never personally met, I have never known of a more remarkable and resolute person than Paul. He was indeed a servant of God. He was someone God used mightily to spread the Word and change lives. It was a singular honor to collaborate with him for the cause of Christ.[4]

---

4. To read more of Priscilla's story, see Witherington, *Priscilla, the Life of an Early Christian* (2019).

IN THE WORDS OF PHOEBE—
PAUL'S FEMALE DEACON

Phoebe is a woman from Cenchreae, a town located five miles southeast of Corinth, on the Aegean coast of Greece. She is mentioned only in Paul's Letter to the Romans, which he wrote while living in Corinth (c. AD 56–58). Apparently, she was quite notable. She is the only woman in the New Testament referred to as a deacon. Although it could simply mean "servant, minister, or messenger" in context, it seems to imply much more. Elsewhere, the term "deacon" refers to men, like Stephen, but Paul says in 1 Timothy 3:11 that the women "likewise are to be worthy of respect."

Romans 16:1–2 reads: "I commend to you our sister Phoebe, a deacon of the church in Cenchreae. I ask you to receive her in the Lord in a way worthy of his people and to give her any help she may need from you, for she has been the benefactor of many people, including me." Most agree that Phoebe was responsible for bringing Paul's letter to the Christian church in Rome.

Icon of Phoebe from the icon workshop at Meteora

I have finally reached Rome. It was not the season for lengthy sailing. I had to trek up to Macedonia, follow the Via Egnatia to Dyrrachium, take the shorter boat ride across the Adriatic to Brindisi on the east coast of Italy, and then hike northwest to Rome itself. I am exhausted! The ninth month in the Roman calendar, what you call November, is no month for travel. But in this case, it was unavoidable. Paul had stressed the urgency of getting his epistle read out in the household assemblies in Rome. But he himself was not to get there for several more years, and then only under the supervision of a Roman centurion who then put him under house arrest! Neither he nor I envisioned this outcome when he and representatives from various Christ-follower assemblies headed off from the port of Cenchreae to Jerusalem, to turn over the collection for the poor followers of Christ there, a collection from various of Paul's Gentile congregations in Achaia, Macedonia, Asia, and Galatia. Life is what happens when you are making other plans or, as Paul would put it, when Satan gets in the way of your mission work!

I am now an old lady living in Rome. I would like to go back to Cenchreae but the travel is probably too much for me now. I arrived in Rome some ten or so years ago with Paul's letter to the household congregations here. It was a time of division within the Christ-follower community, not least because many of the Jewish followers of Christ, particularly their leaders like Priscilla and Aquila, had been sent into exile by Claudius for causing disturbances in the synagogues there. Luke wrote about it in Acts 18. As it turned out, I would not have known Priscilla and Aquila had they not fled to Corinth and set up their new home and tent-making business in Corinth.

Cenchreae is a small fishing village on the east side of Corinth and the Isthmus. There I had my home. When Paul was in Corinth for a while, and after his trial before Gallio, he ended up staying at my villa on the coast. I was sufficiently far away from Corinth that Paul would be out of sight and out of mind most of the time. We had established there a small meeting of Christ followers in my house, and Paul named me a *diakonos,* a deacon. He said I was the first woman he had designated to that role and I was honored. While the term sometimes means a person who waits on tables, in its broader sense it refers to anyone who provides needed practical service in some enterprise. And that I could certainly do.

I was a businesswoman for many decades. My business was making *garum,* the fermented fish pickle sauce loved so much throughout the empire. I had fishermen, fermenters, and amphorae makers in my employ. It was a very good business indeed. I had boats shipping amphorae of this relish especially around the Aegean but also to Rome. Despite lots of competition in Rome, I made good money there from my specialty sauces. I came up with the idea of fermenting the little bits of fish in several different ways and adding several different spices. Thus, I became not only prosperous but a woman of independent means, a rarity in my world. While I was still in my twenties, my husband died in a shipwreck heading to Melita with some of our *garum*. I never remarried.

When Paul came to Corinth, I heard him speak at the home of Erastus. It was indeed a life-changing experience. I was minimally religious prior to that time, but I was in a period of my life where I was searching for meaning and purpose beyond just doing business with the world. I was lonely and some things about life in Greece frightened me, not least being the Roman takeover of the legal system in Corinth. But then that had happened well before my time, when the Romans razed the city and turned it into a Roman colony town where Roman soldiers mustered out and got land and a pension.[1]

When I got to Rome, Paul had a letter of introduction for me, which I could show to the household assemblies. He asked them to give me whatever support I needed. But my main task was to go from household to household reading out Paul's lengthy discourse and then exhorting the Gentiles to accept and embraces the Jewish followers of Christ with every show of affection and welcome. Paul was hoping to unite the two differing groups and reduce the amount of Gentile prejudice against Jews before he arrived. And I would say to some extent he succeeded.

As it happened, many Jews including even some of Paul's relatives and apostolic co-workers had come to Rome to further the gospel here. This included Andronicus and Junia, Priscilla and Aquila, and various people from Asia, such as Epenetus, the first convert from that region. It also included Rufus, the son of the man who actually carried the cross for Jesus to Golgotha, Simon from Cyrenica. Paul, after his conversion, had stayed with Rufus's mother in Jerusalem when he was not very welcome elsewhere. She played very much the same role as I have for Paul, namely

---

1. In 146 BC the Roman general Lucius Mummius crushed the Achaean Confederacy, including capturing and destroying ancient Corinth. A century later in 44 BC Julius Caesar rebuilt Corinth as a Roman city on top of the old city grid, and renamed the city "Colonia Laus Iulia Corinthiensis," which was to say Julius's Corinthian colony. Thereafter it was a Roman colony city, serving Rome's purposes to have cities throughout out the empire run like miniature Romes with Roman laws.

being a patroness. The strategy was to get a large contingent of Christ followers in Rome to penetrate the upper echelons of society. To some degree this had already happened by the time I got to Rome. There was Herodion, a descendent of the Herods, who was educated in Rome, and there were slaves in the emperor's own household who had become Christ followers. But much more needed to be done.

And then there were reprisals. After the fire in Rome, which destroyed whole districts of the city, Christ followers were blamed. Both Paul and then Peter were executed, as were various ordinary Christians in the Circus Maximus.[2] They were set afire! Now we have meetings even in the catacombs but, fortunately, Nero is no longer with us—apparently he took his own life. Things are more stable now with the Flavians ruling the empire.

This last happened by a strange means. Josephus, a Jewish historian who lives here in Rome, was at one time a Jewish general fighting against Vespasian's forces during the Jewish wars, which have now ended with the disastrous destruction of the temple in Jerusalem. Josephus surrendered and, in a surprise move, prophesied that Vespasian would become the new emperor. So, his troops declared this a true prophecy and soon enough, after the chaos of the year of three emperors, Vespasian returned to Rome and was recognized as the emperor! Josephus was set up as a prophet and a historian here in Rome. Needless to say, many Jews see Josephus as a traitor, especially the Jewish zealots leading the fight against Rome. But he is now safely ensconced in Rome, far from the madding crowd in Judaea.

Vespasian has restored order in Rome and elsewhere. Things are much quieter for us. There have been no persecutions in the last year or so. Nevertheless, we have chosen to meet not just in homes but also in the catacombs. Partly this is because we believe that the martyrs who have gone before us into paradise are still very much alive. We have the opportunity to worship with them if we do it in that place where they seem so close. There are even now wall paintings of the saints starting to show up in the catacombs.

---

2. Not in the Colosseum, which did not exist until Titus built it in the 70s. Titus not only had built his triumphal arch with pictures of the booty taken from the temple in Jerusalem, he also enslaved various Jews, bringing them back to Rome and they built the Colosseum which was erected in the 70s near that arch.

This is the earliest painting of the raising of Lazarus by Jesus found in Rome's Callixtus catacomb. Notice that Jesus is depicted as a Roman with short hair and a toga.

https://www.christianiconography.info/lazarus.html.

Jesus as the good shepherd is a painting in the catacombs. Jesus is not depicted as a Jew but rather someone looking more like a Roman. These catacomb paintings likely come from a slightly later period than the first century, possible from during the time of the Decian and Diocletian persecutions.

Jesus as the Good Shepherd, mid-3rd century.
Callixtuscatacomb, Rome.

https://www.bibleodyssey.org/en/tools/image-gallery/s/shepherd-werlin.

There is so much more I could say, but in regard to Paul himself, he made us understand that the good news of salvation through and in Christ was for all of humanity. Further, he demonstrated that the gospel could be indigenized in any culture. He once said that we were the heralds of the first genuinely evangelistic religion and that all of us were missionaries in God's service. It was this high calling that I responded to, found meaning and purpose in, and to which I have devoted the last almost twenty years of my life. It has not been without loss, trials, and tribulations, but even the martyrdom of some Christ followers did not snuff out the movement. Instead, it showed the courage and bravery of our people defending our faith. And this only led to more converts. Thanks be to God.

IN THE WORDS OF FELIX—
PAUL'S PROCURATOR AND JAILER

Marcus Antonius Felix was the Roman procurator in Judaea from AD 52 to 58. Felix was a Greek, a freedman thanks to either Claudius or Claudius's mother, Antonia Minor. According to Tacitus, Felix and his brother Pallas were descended from the Greek kings of Arcadia.

Unfortunately, Felix was a cruel procurator, easily bribed (Acts 24:26) and quick to put down any disturbances in his realm. His most ardent opponent was the high priest Jonathan, so in AD 58, Felix had him assassinated. Paul himself stood trial before Felix in the port city of Caesarea. Both Felix and his wife Drusilla heard Paul preach and invited him to talk with them further. True to his nature, however, Felix tried to bribe Paul (Acts 24:24–26)! When that didn't work, Felix imprisoned Paul for two years (Act 24:27).

Image published in 1553 by Guillaume Rouille (c. 1518–1589). Public Domain.

ENCOUNTERS WITH PAUL

Two sides of two different bronze Hebrew coins (*prutah*, pl. *prutot*) minted by Felix. At best ten *prutot* would buy a loaf of bread. Felix followed the lead of Pilate and others by not making coins with images of emperors. On the right coin, note the Roman *fiscus*, a legal symbol, on one side, and the palm or pomegranate tree on the other side.

I am Marcus Antonius Felix, named for the famous Marc Antony. I was the fourth proconsul sent to that gods-forsaken province called Judaea. If you ask me, this territory should never have been separated from the province of Syria, but that ship sailed decades ago during the time of Augustus and his successor Tiberius. To say this is not a plum appointment is putting things mildly. The weather is inclement; the people are religious fanatics; and the territory is notoriously hard to govern. I have been stuck here for almost six years! Only Pontius Pilatus lasted longer. In my earlier life I was a Greek freedman who served at the pleasure of Claudius's mother, who was indeed a daughter of Marc Antony. I've been here so long, I've gone through two rounds of making coins for the locals. I have to watch my step, now that I secretly had Jonathan the high priest assassinated. I got tired of his criticism of my regime. He claimed I am corrupt and cruel. Imagine that!

You ask me about this man Saul of Tarsus, who goes by Paul now. He has been under house arrest for several years now. An odd fellow, he is not susceptible to a bribe to get released, unlike other Jews I've dealt with for the last several years. Since he is a Roman citizen, I can't torture him for any reason. All he wants to do is talk about this dead Jew named Jesus whom Pilate executed over twenty years ago. Paul claims some "god" raised him from the dead! Why would the dead want to come back to this world full of disease, decay, and death? It doesn't make much sense.

I have to admit, Paul was quite the talker and I enjoyed some of the conversation we had. He usually droned on about salvation through the Jew named Jesus, but the last time my wife, Druscilla, and I talked with him was different. He began talking about righteousness and self-control and

IN THE WORDS OF FELIX—PAUL'S PROCURATOR AND JAILER

the coming judgment on wickedness. Frankly, it unnerved me. I dismissed him saying, "That's enough for now! You may leave. When I find it convenient, I will send for you." I was still hoping for a bribe from Paul, but it was not forthcoming. Druscilla explained to me that these new Jesus followers believed that their god was a god who did bring justice and judgment to the world, especially in the case of corrupt leaders. I didn't want to hear any more about that, so I left Paul under house arrest and let the next proconsul, whom I hear will be Festus, deal with him—one less headache for me.

These Jews are hard to figure out. Many of them will not compromise, be dishonest, change their beliefs, or just be reasonable to get ahead in life. Paul is exhibit A for Jewish stubbornness. A courageous man, he was prepared to stand up to a mob in Jerusalem. He was not afraid to claim his rights as a Roman citizen for Roman, not Jewish, justice. There is something admirable about this, but also foolhardy. I'm glad I will not have to deal with Paul much longer.

IN THE WORDS OF JAMES, BROTHER OF JESUS—THE CHRISTIANS' SPIRITUAL LEADER IN JERUSALEM

James (Latin *Jacobus*; Hebrew *Ya'akov*) was a brother of Jesus. Roman Catholicism and Eastern Orthodoxy teach that James was not one of Mary's biological children, but rather a stepbrother as a son of Joseph from an earlier marriage, or even a cousin. But Protestants believe that Mary had more children after Jesus; indeed, Mark mentions four brothers, including James (Mark 6:3) and also sisters. Although never one of the twelve apostles, James became leader of the Jerusalem church after the death of Jesus. As recorded by Eusebius, Clement of Alexandria related that, "This James, whom the people of old called The Just because of his outstanding virtue, was the first . . . to be elected to the episcopal throne of the Jerusalem church."[1] Paul in his epistles (Gal 1:18–19, 2:9; 1 Cor 15:3–80) and Luke in his book of Acts (15:13–21) both portray James as a leader in the Jerusalem church. Paul delivers money raised for the Jerusalem community to James. Paul abides with the Jerusalem Council's decision, which was formulated by James around AD 50 (see Acts 15).

Icon of Eusebius from the icon workshop at Meteora.

Traditionally, the book of James is attributed to James the Just, brother of Jesus. And tradition says James was stoned to death by the Pharisees, at the instigation of the grandson of Caiaphas who was then high priest in c. AD 62, though there is also a tradition he was thrown from the pinnacle of the temple.

---

1. Eusebius, *Ecclesiastical History*, Book 1.1; Clement, *Outlines*, Book 6.

IN THE WORDS OF JAMES, BROTHER OF JESUS

My older brother, Yeshua, was an enigma. Yes, I knew he could perform miracles and exorcisms but frankly we weren't looking for a messiah who did those things. We expected a Davidic figure who reestablished the monarchy so we could be ruled by our own people. David performed no miracles and my brother had no political ambitions. At one point we were afraid for his sanity and life. When we heard about some of the things he was doing like exorcisms we tried to bring him home. Literally, we thought he was out of his mind. But our brother continued preaching in the synagogues and stirring up the people.

At best I believed he was like Elijah or other northern prophets who performed miracles. After all, our cousin John was a well-known prophetic figure, an action prophet. Maybe brother Yeshua was the same sort of figure. He spoke of himself *in the third person* as **the** Son of Man, presumably referring to the figure in the vision in Daniel. Whoever that mysterious figure was or is, he didn't seem to be an anointed king in the line of David.

What changed, you ask? My brother Yeshua appeared to me after his crucifixion! I had to totally reevaluate his life, ministry, death, and believe in resurrection! The fact was that God vindicated him beyond death. His physical appearances to us were undeniable proof that he was the risen Lord. The Scriptures were not pointing to a warrior king, but a servant leader. And this led me to reevaluate my life as well. And then along came Paul!

As if understanding my brother was not difficult enough, Saul of Tarsus, the persecutor of those of us who followed my brother, claimed to have just as much of a miraculous change in his life as I had gone through when I saw the risen Yeshua. But here's the problem. Yeshua appeared to the disciples and to me during a forty-day period after his resurrection. Then, like Elijah, he ascended into heaven. Here was Saul, years later claiming he had a vision of the risen Yeshua as he was heading to Damascus to take more Christ followers prisoner! And this after he had stood as a witness to Stephen's stoning.

Were we really supposed to believe that Saul had changed dramatically and was now on our side? Or was he a sly person trying to worm his way into our inner circle so he could destroy us? Any number of us had severe doubts about him. We first sent him home to Tarsus. We would wait to see if there was any evidence not only that he had really changed but also that he was called to be the Apostle to the Gentiles. I have to confess that our later private meeting with him certainly convinced Peter that Saul was to be trusted. On the strength of that endorsement we gave him the right hand of fellowship.

And there was Titus. There was no denying that Titus had committed himself, at great personal cost, to be a follower of Yeshua. However, Saul insisted Titus did not need to be circumcised and become a Jew to be a Christ follower. Some among us didn't like that notion at all because it meant the Way, as we called it, would not be seen as just another sect or movement within Judaism. I confess I was not sure how this would all work out.

So, Paul, as he was now being called, Titus, Barnabas, and others were witnessing to non-Jews or Gentiles. Peter and his co-workers were sharing the good news with Jews. To be honest, when Yeshua said we should go make disciples in the nations, some of us assumed he meant to share our messianic message with our fellow Jews in the diaspora. In fact, I wrote a sermon for the diaspora Jews after many became followers of Yeshua.[2]

Some of our stricter Pharisaic followers of Jesus did not like the endorsement of Paul and his approach to evangelism. They heard rumors about what was going on in Galatia and even Antioch. I gave them permission to go and check things out. They, however, had their own agenda beyond just finding out the facts. They decided to exhort Paul's recent converts to get circumcised and keep the Mosaic covenant. Clearly, we needed to have a general meeting of all the leaders to sort these matters out, but it was not to happen until almost twenty years after Yeshua was crucified. More and more Gentiles were committing themselves to the Way. We desperately needed to find a common path forward.

Finally, we gathered in Jerusalem. The Pharisaic followers kept insisting that Gentiles must become Jews to be part of the Way. I knew that was problematic but wanted all the various viewpoints to have their say before making a ruling. No one could deny that there were some remarkable conversion stories involving Gentiles. But on what basis could there be unity between all these followers of Yeshua? Paul was unusually silent when the suggestion was made that Gentiles must become full-fledged Jews.

Then, surprisingly, Peter stood up and made this impassioned short speech:

> Brothers, you know that some time ago God made a choice among you that the Gentiles might hear from my lips the message of the gospel and believe. God, who knows the heart, showed that he accepted them by giving the Holy Spirit to them, just as he did to us. He did not discriminate between us and them, for he purified

---

2. Most scholars believe that James, the brother of Jesus, is the author of the Epistle of James.

their hearts by faith. Now then, why do you try to test God by putting on the necks of Gentiles a yoke that neither we nor our ancestors have been able to bear? No! We believe it is through the grace of our Lord Jesus that we are saved, just as they are.

To say this was a surprising speech is an understatement. There was stunned silence! After this, Paul and Barnabas gave their report about the success among the Gentiles. One could sense that God's spirit was leading the conversation in a particular direction. I felt led to see if I could connect the Way to the more traditional hopes of reviving the Davidic monarchy. I paraphrased some statements from Amos 9:11–12 as follows:

> After this I will return and rebuild David's fallen tent.
> Its ruins I will rebuild, and I will restore it,
> that the rest of humankind may seek the Lord,
> even all the Gentiles who bear my name,
> says the Lord who does these things known from long ago.[3]

Then, I knew they were all looking to me to bring this to a resolution. I made clear we were not going to impose the whole Mosaic law on Gentiles. Instead, there would be a focus on the essential and central commands to avoid idolatry and immorality as Moses said so clearly. This would prevent the Gentiles from being considered infidels in the diaspora synagogues.

The Gentiles must stay away from pagan temple dinners where the god was thought to be dining with the participants and where there would be present food offered to the god (*eidolothuton*), in the form of his idol, as well as blood, things strangled (i.e., birds), and sexual immorality. All these things often accompanied those feasts, which sometimes degenerated into orgies. This is unacceptable. When the decree was read to the Gentiles, Paul reminded his converts that they had turned away from idols to the one true God.

Later I learned that Paul implemented the decree in Corinth, where there was a regular tendency of the socially elite members of a house church to go to idol feasts at the temple of Asclepius or the temple of Aphrodite up on the Acro-Corinth. Silas went with Paul to explain these things to Jews and Gentiles who might not be sure the decree against idol feasts came from the Jerusalem church!

On Paul's prior visit to our private meeting, I asked him to have his congregations take up a collection for the poor in Jerusalem. We were

---

3. See also Acts 15:13–18.

suffering financially from not being allowed to draw on the city dole. Even our widows and orphans were denied help, so we had to take care of our own folk on the margins of our community. Paul was happy to do this. He solicited a lot of money from his household congregations. Unfortunately, this money did not come to us until a decade later, when trouble was already brewing that led to the Jewish war with Rome in Galilee and Judaea.

The situation in Jerusalem was tense. While Paul hoped that this collection would help bind together the more Gentile Pauline congregations with those of us centered in Jerusalem, alas, there was still too much animosity among Jews against Gentiles in general and Romans in particular. Some of Paul's more elite converts were Romans, like Erastus in Corinth. Some of the Jerusalem community saw the money as a sort of bribe to accept Gentile congregations! I urged Paul when he came with the funds to use some of the money to support Nazaritic vows. He did so but, when he went to the temple, he was accused of taking a Gentile into the Jews-only zone, which I am sure he didn't do. Nevertheless, a riot ensued and he was taken prisoner by a Roman soldier from the Antonia Fortress.

At present he has been under house arrest in Caesarea Maritima for some time, awaiting the resolution of his case. He has put up with two procurators, Felix and now Festus. The word which just came to me is that Paul has appealed to have his case heard by the Emperor Nero. This means he will have to be transported to Rome. We did not intervene in this process for the very good reason as it would have accomplished nothing. In the eyes of the Roman procurator, we have no legal status compared to the representatives of the Sanhedrin. We knew that Paul could remind the authorities that he was a Roman citizen and demand Roman justice. Smart man!

I hear that Nero is basically an absentee emperor, running around the empire reading his poetry and playing the lyre at various contests at the games in Corinth and Olympia. Perhaps his supervisors, Seneca and Burrus, will take the usual line and find in favor of Paul as a Roman citizen. In any case, were the Sanhedrin wanting to really pursue the matter, they would have to go all the way to Rome to appear and bear witness against Paul. Right now, they have their hands full here with the Zealots! A long trek to Rome seems unlikely. We will keep praying for Paul's release.

I am now left alone in charge of the Way in Jerusalem. Peter has gone off to Pontus and Bithynia; Barnabas is back on Kypros (Cyprus); and Silas is with Paul. The only way I keep the peace is by continuing to be Torah true as a good witness to my fellow Jews. They call me James the Just. But when I ponder the direction our movement is going, especially in light of the Pauline successes with Gentiles plus troubles here with my fellow Jews, it appears that the future of the movement lies with increasing the Gentile members. For the most part, tragically, Jews in the diaspora have rejected the good news shared by Paul and Peter and others.

So, I must watch and pray and see what happens through the providence of our God. I fear war is coming again to our land. I must keep my focus on our community and its survival. God help us in the coming days.[4]

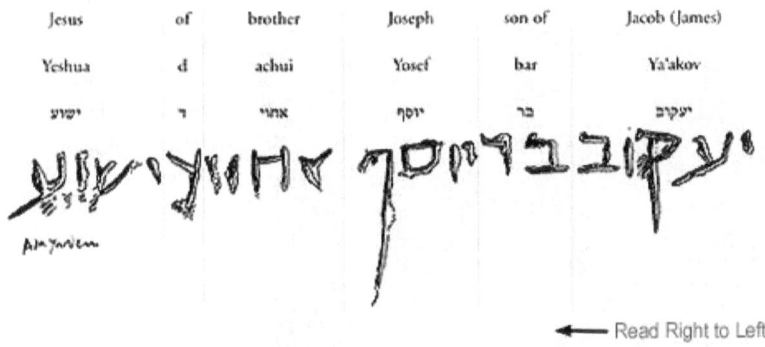

← Read Right to Left

The ossuary in which James was likely buried in AD 63.
The inscription is honorific and reads: "James, son of Joseph, brother of Jesus."
Only one other period ossuary mentions a brother.
http://www.centuryone.com/ossuary.html.

---

4. James was martyred at the hands of the Jewish authority before the full Jewish war was underway in AD 62. A descendant of the family of Annas and Caiaphas, who turned Jesus over to Pilate, had James executed and another of the community members named Simeon was to carry the leadership forward. This means that James was martyred before either Paul or Peter, who died in Rome after the fire in AD 64.

IN THE WORDS OF TIMOTHY—
PAUL'S BEST FRIEND

Timothy was brought up in Lystra, in what is now the country of Turkey. His father was Greek. In 2 Timothy 1:5 we learn that his mother Eunice and grandmother Lois, both Jewish converts to Christianity, were noted for their faith. Thus, Timothy grew up in the faith. Since his father was Greek, Timothy had not been circumcised. Despite the ruling made at the Council of Jerusalem, Paul saw to it that Timothy was circumcised to ensure his acceptance by the local Jews. Around AD 52, Timothy joined Paul and Silas on the second missionary journey. At one point Paul went to Athens while Silas and Timothy went back to Thessalonike to check on the new converts, before they all rendezvoused in Corinth. In 1 Corinthians 16:10,

Willem Drost (1633–1659) *Timothy with his Grandmother Lois.* Hermitage Museum, St. Petersburg.

IN THE WORDS OF TIMOTHY—PAUL'S BEST FRIEND

Paul will ask the Corinthians to be kind to Timothy because he is doing the Lord's work. It seems that much of the time Timothy traveled back and forth across the Aegean between Corinth in Greece and Ephesus in Turkey. Timothy appears as the coauthor of 2 Corinthians, Philippians, Colossians, 1 and 2 Thessalonians, and Philemon. It seems that Paul and Timothy were inseparable to the end in Rome. Paul says, "I have no one like him . . ." (Phil 2:20). Tradition indicates that Timothy eventually became bishop of Ephesus, where he was stoned to death in AD 97.

My mother Eunice and my grandmother Lois were Jewish and became early followers of the Christ thanks to the ministry of Paul in Lystra. My father was Greek and did not practice any religion. I was a young man when Paul and Barnabas first came to Lystra and healed someone. At that time, the elders remembered the story of when Zeus and Hermes had come to Lystra in disguise and were only welcomed by an elderly couple, whom they richly blessed, leaving the rest of the city out of such blessings. This story is vividly told in Ovid's *Metamorphosis*. In light of it, the city fathers thought Barnabas must be Zeus and Paul must be Hermes! The elders went all out to honor them with a sacrifice of a sacred bull. But Paul and Barnabas did not know the Lystran language so they did not know what was happening until the proceedings were already in motion. When they finally found out by asking questions in Greek, they tried to stop the pagan celebration. Needless to say, this rebuff was not taken well by the city fathers, who did not like being publicly shamed. Right about then some Jews from western Galatia showed up seeking to harm Paul and Barnabas. They won the crowd over and stoned Paul! He recovered and the next morning they left for Derbe as quickly as possible. These are just some of the stories my grandmother told me.

It was on his second trip through Galatia that Paul stopped again in Lystra. He recruited me to be one of his co-workers for many reasons. Since he was still visiting synagogues with the good news first, he thought I could help with the Jewish audience if he circumcised me. So, I was circumcised by Paul. I was exhibit A to show that Paul still revered the laws of Moses.

I then began to travel with Paul and Silas, heading west to Macedonia and then Greece. I was literate and could write as well as read Greek quite fluidly. For this reason, I helped with the composition of several of Paul's letters after the second missionary journey—letters to the Thessalonians, one letter each to the Corinthians, the Philippians, the Colossians, and the more personal letter to Philemon. Paul wanted to make clear that he was not acting alone when he gave imperatives and apostolic mandates.

I must say that Paul invested a lot of time and trust in me, more than I thought I deserved. And near the end of his ministry, I was shocked when he left me in charge of the household congregations in Ephesos. He had worked so hard to build up these house churches over the course of more than three years. I read the letter sent to the Philippians, where he said of me, "I have no one like Timothy." I was never a bold or outgoing person. Indeed, I was rather shy and timid, more prone to reading than vigorous activity, more a supporter than a leader.

If I had one good quality, I would say I was loyal to a fault. Near the end of Paul's life, he summoned me to Rome. Paul wanted to see me once more. He wrote two very personal letters to me near the end, the first with instructions for dealing with Ephesos and the issues there. The second was more personal, and I can hardly reread that one without weeping.

There was no one else quite like Paul—a dynamo of energy, purpose, and zeal for the Lord. Many times, I could not understand where he found the strength to do a lot of what he did, especially after being jailed, beaten, run out of towns, stoned, taken to court, and much more. But he would always say that God's power was made perfect in his weakness, and God's grace was sufficient for him to complete his tasks. My very last task was taking the parchments all the way to Rome, for I had the master copies of the letters sent to various household congregations in the empire.

When I arrived in Rome, I was too late. Paul had just been beheaded. I learned this from Luke, who actually composed those letters to me and Titus. I had noticed the style of those three letters was different but it had not registered until then. Luke was with Paul at the last and Paul was brave to the last. As he said, he had fought the good fight, run the good race, and finished the course. When he said things like "be imitators of me as I am of Christ," in my heart I always said, I could never do all that! Nevertheless, I tried to approximate his zeal and dedication. I was recently jailed like Paul had been in Philippi, but was released on that occasion, and traveled with Apollos to Rome to see the wavering Jewish followers of Christ there.

Now, I am rather old. I am the *episcopos* or overseer of various household congregations. I do not travel as much as when I was younger, but I have been encouraged to see these congregations continue to grow and thrive despite the loss of our great leaders, Paul and Peter. Clement has taken on the mantle of overseeing congregations in Rome. He recently

IN THE WORDS OF TIMOTHY—PAUL'S BEST FRIEND

wrote to the Corinthians. He wanted to follow up on some of the ideas Paul had laid out in his famous Letter to the Corinthians.

I suppose I should start writing to some of the congregations I have served like the ones in Ephesos, but I lack the eloquence and rhetorical skills of Paul or Apollos. Nevertheless, I will try.

When I look back on my life, it has been quite an adventure with more than a little danger involved. But it has been worth it all, for the good news about Christ and his salvation has spread right across the empire, from Jerusalem to Rome and beyond to Hispania. I could never have foreseen all this happening when I first joined Paul more than thirty years ago. In the end, what Paul often preached and wrote to the Romans is true—God works all things together for good for those who love him and are called according to purpose. In my heart I know this is true and every day I re-read the words he wrote to me in his second letter: "I remind you to fan into flame the gift of God, which is in you through the laying on of my hands." In his very last letter to me I can still hear his God-whispered words. Some days I ask myself, where would I be today had he not picked me as his constant companion and co-worker? I cannot answer that question.

IN THE WORDS OF KING HEROD AGRIPPA II—PAUL'S NEMESIS

Marcus Julius Agrippa II (King Herod Agrippa II) was born c. AD 27/28. His father was Herod Agrippa 1 (11 BC to AD 44) of Acts 12 fame, who persecuted the followers of Jesus, killed James the son of Zebedee, and jailed Peter. At the end of Acts 12, however, Herod Agrippa I is smitten with disease by God and dies in AD 44 in Caesarea.

Herod Agrippa II, being only seventeen when his father died, stayed in Rome until the Emperor Claudius finally sent him back to Israel in AD 48. Over the years he gained more territory and by AD 55 he was officially King Herod Agrippa II, the last of the Herodian dynasty, which began with his great-grandfather, Herod the Great.

Meanwhile, under Felix, the local procurator in Judaea, Paul was placed under house arrest with a Roman guard in Caesarea, as reported in Acts 24. Portius Festus succeeded Felix c. AD 59. As reported in Acts 25, Paul was brought before Festus and requested to be sent to Rome. Festus famously declared, "You have appealed to Caesar—to Caesar you will go!" But King Agrippa and Berenice arrived to pay their respects to Festus and they all discussed Paul's case. Acts 26 records the meeting between Paul, Agrippa, his sister Berenice, and Portius Festus. The transcript of the trial is included here.

In AD 65 Agrippa tried to avert the Jewish rebellion but failed. In AD 66 he and Berenice were expelled from Jerusalem. Between AD 66 and 73 Agrippa took Rome's side in the struggle, sending two thousand men to support Vespasian's suppression. After Jerusalem fell, he went to Rome, was made a praetor, and given more territory to rule. While in Rome he was a friend and a major source for Josephus' famous chronicle called *The Antiquities of the Jews*.

IN THE WORDS OF KING HEROD AGRIPPA II—PAUL'S NEMESIS

Published by Guillaume Rouille (c.1518-1589).
"Promptuarii Iconum Insigniorum."

I am the last of the Herodian rulers in this land. My legal name is Marcus Julius Agrippa. I was educated in Rome and befriended by the Emperor Claudius. Porcius Festus has become the procurator of Judaea. My sister, Berenice, and I decided to visit him at Caesarea Maritima, a magnificent port built by my ancestor Herod the Great.

I do know Festus was intrigued by the Jew named Paul but he didn't know quite what to make of him, not least because he was also a Roman citizen. Festus was not inclined to render a negative judgment against him. But Festus asked me to help understand what the real issues were in this case. He was mystified by the notion of a Jew proclaiming that another crucified Jew, named Jesus, rose from the dead! This Paul calls him the Messiah and King of the Jews. So, I was brought in to hear his testimony and I gave him permission to speak. I'm just going to cite most of the transcript, so that I don't misrepresent Paul's words.

> King Agrippa, I consider myself fortunate to stand before you today as I make my defense against all the accusations of the Jews, and especially so because you are well acquainted with all the Jewish customs and controversies. Therefore, I beg you to listen to me patiently.
>
> The Jewish people all know the way I have lived ever since I was a child, from the beginning of my life in my own country, and also in Jerusalem. They have known me for a long time and can testify, if they are willing, that I conformed to the strictest

sect of our religion, living as a Pharisee. And now it is because of my hope in what God has promised our ancestors that I am on trial today. This is the promise our twelve tribes are hoping to see fulfilled as they earnestly serve God day and night. King Agrippa, it is because of this hope that these Jews are accusing me. Why should any of you consider it incredible that God raises the dead?

I too was convinced that I ought to do all that was possible to oppose the name of Jesus of Nazareth. And that is just what I did in Jerusalem. On the authority of the chief priests, I put many of the Lord's people in prison, and when they were put to death, I cast my vote against them. Many a time I went from one synagogue to another to have them punished, and I tried to force them to blaspheme. I was so obsessed with persecuting them that I even hunted them down in foreign cities.

On one of these journeys I was going to Damascus with the authority and commission of the chief priests. About noon, King Agrippa, as I was on the road, I saw a light from heaven, brighter than the sun, blazing around me and my companions. We all fell to the ground, and I heard a voice saying to me in Aramaic, "Saul, Saul, why do you persecute me? It is hard for you to kick against the goads." Then I asked, "Who are you, Lord?" "I am Jesus, whom you are persecuting," the Lord replied. "Now get up and stand on your feet. I have appeared to you to appoint you as a servant and as a witness of what you have seen and will see of me. I will rescue you from your own people and from the Gentiles. I am sending you to them to open their eyes and turn them from darkness to light, and from the power of Satan to God, so that they may receive forgiveness of sins and a place among those who are sanctified by faith in me."

So then, King Agrippa, I was not disobedient to the vision from heaven. First to those in Damascus, then to those in Jerusalem and in all Judaea, and then to the Gentiles, I preached that they should repent and turn to God and demonstrate their repentance by their deeds. That is why some Jews seized me in the temple courts and tried to kill me. But God has helped me to this very day; so, I stand here and testify to small and great alike. I am saying nothing beyond what the prophets and Moses said would happen—that the Messiah would suffer and, as the first to rise from the dead, would bring the message of light to his own people and to the Gentiles.

All of us listened respectfully up to this point. But Festus interrupted and shouted, "You are out of your mind, Paul! Your great learning is driving

IN THE WORDS OF KING HEROD AGRIPPA II—PAUL'S NEMESIS

you insane." I was surprised when Paul calmly replied to this outburst by saying, "I am not insane, most excellent Festus. What I am saying is true and reasonable. The king is familiar with these things, and I can speak freely to him. I am convinced that none of this has escaped his notice, because it was not done in a corner. King Agrippa, do you believe the prophets? I know you do!" At this point I was on the hot seat. I tried to lighten the mood by saying, "Do you think that in such a short time you can persuade me to be a Christian?" Undeterred and smiling, Paul replied, "Short time or long—I pray to God that not only you but all who are listening to me today may become what I am, except for these chains!"

I must admit I was impressed with his eloquence and sense of humor. I agreed with Festus that this man could have been set free if had not appealed to Caesar. Personally, if you ask me if I thought Paul was insane, I did not. Jews have different ideas about the messiah and the majority of Jews agree with the Pharisees that resurrection of the dead can and does happen when God so wills.

One had to admire Paul's courage and confidence in his beliefs. I saw no fear in the man when he gave his testimony even after being under house arrest for two years. From what I hear, the stories about his life and trials and tribulations read like a Greek play, a tragedy by Sophocles. One part of me admired the man, though I did not share his beliefs in his Messiah.

I had some trepidation that he might be belligerent, but he was very respectful and knowledgeable. He knew that I knew very well all the sects of Judaism with their permutations and combinations of religious beliefs and practices. It's a pity that he appealed to Nero. Who knows what that quixotic young man may conclude if and when he hears Paul's case. Rumor has it that Nero leaves all the legal matters to Burrus, the head of the Praetorian Guard. I must now turn my attention to more important matters, namely trying to persuade my fellow Jews not to go into open rebellion against Roman rule.

Apostle Paul On Trial, by Nikolai Bodareysky, 1875. Note that Agrippa II, Berenice, his sister, and Festus are seated on thrones.

IN THE WORDS OF JULIUS THE CENTURION—PAUL'S ESCORT TO ROME

Julius the Centurion was a member of the Augustus band or cohort of Roman auxiliaries in Syria during most of the first century. He was assigned to make sure that Paul, a Roman citizen, made it safely to Rome for trial. Aristarchus, a Macedonian from Thessaloniki, also accompanied the group. The fourth was the "we" narrator believed to be Luke, Paul's physician and author of the book of Acts. The first ship that they boarded in Caesarea Maritima came from Adramyttium. Later they changed to a grain ship out of Alexandria Egypt. By now, Paul and his companions were seasoned travelers on land and sea. Paul was in shipwreck before this final voyage (2 Cor 11:25).

A sketch of a larger sailing boat, closer to the size of the grain freighter Paul would have taken from Caesarea Maritima as a prisoner of Rome.

ENCOUNTERS WITH PAUL

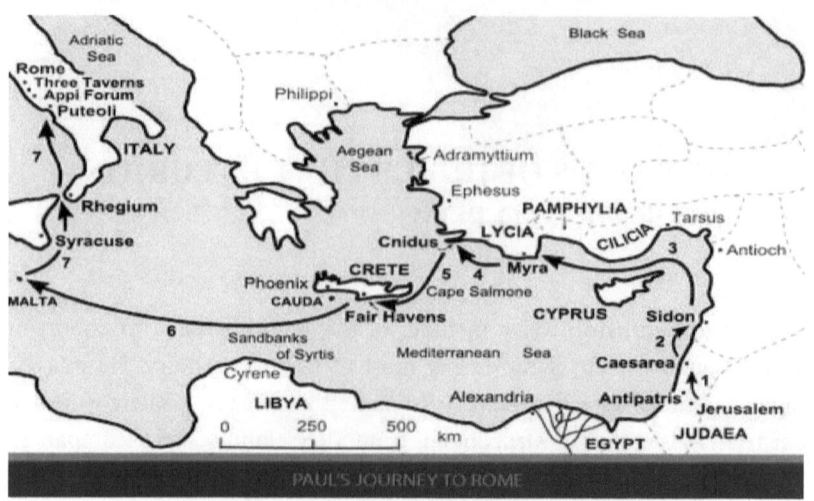

Paul's circuitous route to Rome as a Roman prisoner.

I am Julius, a centurion, part of an imperial unit that served under Herod Agrippa II in Batanea, which he ruled. Agrippa assigned me the task, with the consent of Festus, to get Paul to Rome for trial. Since Paul was not a condemned man, and since he was a Roman citizen, I treated him with utmost respect, unlike the other prisoners on this voyage who were already condemned. It took me a while to find a large boat that would take us and other civilian passengers, over 250 in all, west through the Mediterranean! We hugged the coast going north and west, our first stop being the large port of Sidon. I allowed Paul and Luke to visit their fellow believers in the Christ in Sidon while our boat remained in port. Paul helped make the journey bearable, as he was an educated man, with interesting tales to tell. To be honest, I liked him! Under other circumstances we might have become good friends. But I had to do my duty.

Paul had brought with him his scribe, or doctor, or both, a man called Luke. Both of these men, though they were not sailors, were seasoned travelers by sea. Paul even confided to me that he had been in three shipwrecks previously! Fear was not his companion on this journey and, as it turned out, there was reason to fear! I was apprehensive about this trip as we were sailing past the time of the normal sailing season and the winds would not be favorable.[1] We encountered wind and heavy seas as we headed towards

---

1. Apart from grain freighters, which could sail in the open sea from Egypt to Rome,

IN THE WORDS OF JULIUS THE CENTURION

Cyprus, hugging the north side of that large island. We made port in Myra on the south coast of Asia and then, with some difficulty, made it to Cnidus near Rhodes. I could tell there was going to be rough sailing from then on. Again, this did not trouble Paul; he believed his god was with him and would protect him. I would see him praying early each morning on the deck of the ship. Each passenger had to provide their own food and supplies. Because Paul was a leatherworker, he had brought a tent that he and Luke could shelter under on the deck. He even invited me to join them one stormy night. This man was kind and generous. I couldn't really understand why someone was prosecuting him for his religion when we live in a pluralistic world with many religions. But I did not pry or probe the matter.

From Cnidus we headed to Crete. The winds were so strong we could not get to the port on the north side of the island at ancient Heraklion. We ended up on the south side of the island in a harbor called Fair Havens. Paul adamantly said that we should stay here and ride out the bad weather and winter storms that were surely coming. But the captain and pilot were determined to go on. Probably there was a bonus waiting for them if they got the journey done before the new year. But, like Paul, I was apprehensive. He surprised me by reassuring us that while the ship would likely have to jettison its cargo, there would no loss of life! I guess he heard this from his god!

As Paul predicted, we got caught in a violent storm for many days. I could not help feeling like I was reliving a portion of the story of Odysseus, which I read when I was young. Again and again, Paul exhorted us to be brave and to jettison all nonessentials. When even the veteran sailors began to panic and tried to get in a dinghy, Paul told me to stop them or otherwise there would be terrible loss of life. Apparently, there is an art to wrecking well on the rocks with minimal human harm. I took his advice seriously! We did survive, crawling up in the bay on the isle of Melita.[2] The ship was lost, but all the passengers were saved. Sometimes the gods judged wicked persons by drowning them in the sea and yet we all survived by taking Paul's advice. I wondered if this meant that Paul was not guilty of any crimes.

When the ship was about to wreck, my fellow soldiers wanted to kill the prisoners but I wanted to spare Paul. So, I ordered my men not to kill

---

smaller boats had to sail from point to point, and the sailing season was recognized to end about the middle of October. This voyage took place later in AD 59.

2. Modern-day Malta.

anyone. Rather, we turned them loose to swim or grab a plank and paddle their way to shore. Thus, as Paul said, no one died. That was a remarkable outcome considering the ferocity of the storm.

Yes, we arrived safely in Melita and the locals welcomed us by building a fire to dry us out and keep us warm. Just when I thought we would get a respite from adventures, suddenly a viper appeared and bit Paul on the hand. Some of the locals cried out, saying he must be a wicked man because though he survived the shipwreck the god of justice dealt him this blow. To everyone's amazement, Paul shook the snake off his hand and was none the worse. The natives backed off—some even thought that Paul was a god! But what happened next was equally surprising.

There was an estate nearby that belonged to Publius, the chief official or governor of Melita. He welcomed us to his home and showed us generous hospitality for three days. His father was sick in bed, suffering from fever and dysentery. Paul went in to see him and, after prayer, placed his hands on him and healed him. When this happened, the rest of the sick on the island came and were cured. They honored us in many ways and we spent the winter months on Melita in pleasant company. When we were ready to sail, they furnished us with supplies. But when the sailing season began again in spring, Paul, Luke, the other prisoners and I booked passage on a large grain freighter named *Castor and Pollux*, bound for Rome.

We sailed northeast, passing Syracuse and Rhegium before tacking carefully between Sicily and the coast of Italy. To my great surprise, there were a large number of Christ followers who met Paul at the pier in Puteoli and welcomed us to Italy. Along with Paul and Luke, I became their guest. I sent the other prisoners on ahead to Rome for trial. In the case of Paul, there was no need to hurry. The trial would await the witnesses from Jerusalem against him—if they ever bothered to show up. While eventually I needed to return to duty with Herod Agrippa II back in Caesarea, I still had a responsibility for Paul until his trial was concluded. So, Paul rented a house and I became his regular house guest. He was visited almost daily by his fellow Christ followers and other Jews as well.

After waiting some two years without any Sanhedrin officials or representatives showing up, a verdict was rendered on behalf of the Roman citizen of *non liquet*, that is, not proved. Paul was a free man again. As I was prepared to make the long journey back to Caesarea Maritima, Paul asked me, "What do you think of this Christ that I preach." I smiled and said, "Remember the words of my superior, Agrippa, when you appeared before

IN THE WORDS OF JULIUS THE CENTURION

him—'Almost you persuade me to become a Christ follower.' Well, I'm still considering doing that, and feel exceedingly fortunate to have made your acquaintance. For now, I must say farewell, and may your god continue to be with you, as he surely was on our arduous journey."

IN THE WORDS OF EUTYCHUS—
PAUL'S FORTUNATE FRIEND

Eutychus was a young man living in Troas. His Greek name means "Fortunate" or "Lucky." Troas was a port city on the northwest Aegean coast of Anatolia (today's Turkey). Paul visited Troas during his second journey on his way to Macedonia (c. 49–52) and again on his third journey (c. 53–58). The setting for this story is the end of Paul's third journey. He left Philippi, crossed the Aegean, and is now in the port of Troas once again for a week. While there he gets the opportunity to preach—and Paul can be long-winded. By now it's midnight. Eutychus, who is sitting in a window, falls asleep and falls three stories to his death. But, fortunately, Paul is there to save him. And Luke the physician is there to document what happened noting that Eutychus was truly dead. This story is related in Acts 20:7–12.

**Paul raises Eutychus to life
Figures de la Bible, published 1728
Gerard Hoet (1648–1733),
illustrator.**

IN THE WORDS OF EUTYCHUS—PAUL'S FORTUNATE FRIEND

Saint Paul bringing Eutychus back to life.
Jacques François Courtin
(1772–1752)
Toulouse Cathedral, France.

https://www.patheos.com/blogs/rogerwolsey/2016/04/eutychus-the-first-young-victim-of-organized-religion

My slave nickname is "Lucky" or "Fortunate." I guess the name fits because one evening in Troas I nodded off while sitting in an open window and fell three stories to the ground! I was pronounced dead by Luke, Paul's physician. Paul, who was preaching to us that night, came racing down the stairs, embraced me, and said, "His life is back in him." This was after they were going to cart me off to the necropolis. So, yes, to be clear, I was dead briefly. Paul brought me back, however, which comforted those who cared about me, including my owner.

But how had I come to fall from the window, you may ask? Well, those small upstairs rooms could be hot in summer, especially with all those lamps lit in the room so people could see the speaker. I worked hard that day, though I was then a young man. My master was demanding but fair and had become more kind since becoming a follower of the one called Christ. He wanted his whole household to become followers of Christ. So, he invited Paul to preach in his upper room. Of course, we were all there since it was our home.

Paul seemed to me a figure larger than life. They called him an apostle, which seemed like a minor god to me. The stories about his miracles, conversions through preaching, miraculous escapes from enemies, prison, beatings, and shipwrecks were amazing and exciting. They sounded like tales from the Iliad! Naturally I would think like that since I live near ancient Troas, where the Trojan war took place. Was he like brave Achilles or perhaps Ajax? Maybe, but Paul was not a soldier, although he called himself a soldier of Christ. His weapons were his words and miracles.

The man fairly radiated Christlike qualities—love, joy, peace, patience, kindness—to a fault. Yes, he also had a temper, but so far as I could see his anger was always a righteous anger, not a selfish anger, not an anger born out of a personal grievance or revenge.

I am no longer a young man. I am thankful that Paul extended my life through the grace that came through him. And most recently, at the urging of Paul, my master Demetrius made me a freedman by pronouncing the formula over my bowed head—"for freedom Christ has set you free." Thanks be to God!

IN THE WORDS OF JUNIA—
PAUL'S FRIEND AND APOSTLE

Junia is the Latin version of Joanna, a Jewish woman. For this reason, most scholars agree that she is the wife of Chuza, who managed the household of Herod Antipas I, the ruler of Galilee. We first hear about Joanna/Junia in Luke 8:1–3: "After this, Jesus traveled about from one town and village to another, proclaiming the good news of the kingdom of God. The Twelve were with him, and also some women who had been cured of evil spirits and diseases: Mary (called Magdalene) from whom seven demons had come out; Joanna the wife of Chuza, the manager of Herod's household, Susanna, and many others. These women were helping to support them out of their own means." Apparently, they were independently wealthy enough support the group.

Depiction of Andronicus and Junia, Church of the Most Holy Savior, Palermo, Sicily. Byzantine.

We next hear of Junia/Joanna in Luke 24:1–10. Alongside Mary Magdalene, she visited the tomb on Easter morning—and found it empty. The risen Jesus instructs the women to tell the twelve apostles and other disciples to meet him in Galilee.

Later in Romans 16:7, Paul tells us that Junia is now a person outstanding among the apostles. Paul says that she was "in Christ" before his conversion and "in prison" during his ministry. The church father Chrysostom marveled at her devotion and agreed—"she would be even counted worthy of the appellation of apostle." (We also learn that she travels with a fellow Jew named Andronicus of Pannonia, which indicates that either that she is traveling with her brother or she is now divorced from Chuza and married to Andronicus.)

First of all, my Hebrew name is Joanna, which in Latin becomes Junia. Other than Peter, I know of no one who has spent as much time with either Jesus or Paul as I did. Beginning in Galilee with my good friend Miryam of Migdal we were the two earliest women to commit to being traveling disciples of Jesus. And yes, we provided supplies and meals along the way for the Twelve and other disciples even as we learned all that Jesus taught.

It was the women, not the men, who were last at the cross, first at the empty tomb, and first to see and proclaim the risen Jesus. Indeed, the whole reason Paul later called me an apostle like himself is because I had indeed seen the risen Lord and was commissioned by him to share the good news. But, you ask, how did I get to this point in my life?

I was the wife of Chuza, the estate manager of Herod Antipas in Galilee. This placed me in a socially elite circle of friends and neighbors. We lived comfortably in Tiberias near the Sea of Galilee. Jesus never came to Tiberias, but he did go to nearby Capernaum or, as we Jews called it, Kefir Nahum, the village of the prophet Nahum. Early on there were stories about Jesus healing the people and exorcizing demons in Capernaum. This intrigued me! There was a God-shaped vacuum inside of me. So, one day I walked along the shore of Galilee to Capernaum to hear this remarkable teacher and healer named after Joshua, the great leader of the Hebrews many centuries ago. Do you know that Yeshua or Joshua means "Yahweh saves"? How very appropriate for this man who was bringing in God's final saving reign on earth.

My marriage to Chuza was an arranged marriage, settled between his father and mine—a marriage of convenience. At first my husband was

IN THE WORDS OF JUNIA—PAUL'S FRIEND AND APOSTLE

too busy managing Herod's lands to care what I was doing in my spare time. Eventually he noticed that I was gone for days at a time! I admitted that I was now a disciple of Yeshua. Remember that this was after John the Baptizer was taken prisoner by Herod and locked up in the fortress of Machaerus across the Jordan. Chuza was not a religious man and he sensed danger in my newfound religious beliefs.

Yes, Herod Antipas was frightened by John but he also saw him as an object of curiosity. When Herod learned that I was a follower of John's cousin, Jesus, who was also some kind of change agent, healer, prophet, he sensed trouble. So, he told Chuza to choose—me or his lucrative job as an estate manager! Naturally, he chose the latter and I was quickly handed my "get" or bill of divorce. Fortunately, I had my dowry and income from my well-to-do family. These resources allowed me to travel with and learn from Jesus and his followers.

The day that Jesus rose from the dead and appeared to me, Mary Magdalene, and several other women, he commissioned us to go tell the brothers the good news that he was alive and well. Of course, they did not believe us because the testimony of a woman was considered suspect. One member of the Twelve, who shall remain nameless, made the rude suggestion that we fantasized seeing him. This really made me angry and Jesus rebuked the men for not believing either the prophets or our testimony!

After the forty-day period of his appearances, we waited until the feast of Pentecost came and God's Spirit fell on us all. I had been going to the meetings in the home of John Mark's mother. It was there that I met Andronicus, a truly godly man, who had been one of the first converts after Peter's speech on Pentecost. Unlike my first marriage, this one turned out to be a love match between two adults and we were wed within a year of Jesus' ascension.

But you also asked about my encounters with Paul. Remember that I was in Jerusalem when Saul, as he was still known then, was working with the Sanhedrin and stood as witness to the stoning of Stephanos. I was more than a little scared of that zealot. Jesus by contrast had preached peace, nonviolence, forgiveness, and even love of enemies. But I must confess, Saul was one enemy it would take divine intervention in my life to love. It would be three more years before I met Saul after his incredible Damascus Road experience.

By then, Andronicus and I had been married for a good while and were sharing the good news in Judaea. When Saul came back to Jerusalem after a period of time in Arabia he had a private session with Peter and James, who sent him off to his home region for awhile. Eventually, I heard him speak to the pillar apostles. I was moved by his testimony and believed he really was a changed man. Besides, trustworthy and true Barnabas had vouched for him, plus there was the testimony of Titus. Saul insisted Titus had been saved by grace and did not need circumcision to be a true follower of Jesus. This was a novel idea to me since I always thought that the Way, as it was called, was simply Judaism at its messianic truest. But Saul was envisioning a new people, Jew and Gentile united in Christ.

Andronicus was in Jerusalem with me and after the meeting, in which Saul, as he was still known then, was authorized to continue to bear witness to Gentiles and Peter to Jews. We asked him if he could use some co-workers. Andronicus and I told Saul our story. Immediately, he saw the value of having co-workers who, especially in my case, had followed Jesus' ministry, witnessed his death, and seen the risen Lord before his ascension. This was the beginning of many exciting years of travel with Saul who, after witnessing to Sergius Paulus on Cyprus, insisted on using the Greek and Latin equivalents of his name, Paulos and Paulus, since he was mainly working with Gentiles. This made good sense and is also why we continued to use our Latin names Andronicus and Junia when we worked with the Apostle to the Gentiles.

While eventually we would end up in Rome working for the gospel, for some years we traveled and worked with Paul and, at one point, we even ended up in jail with him in Macedonia. There is so much more I could tell you about this man, but I will leave you with this thought. There are some whose enthusiasm for God's calling in their life is so strong that it affects and infects others to share that zeal and enthusiasm. You get caught up in the vision of working for God with someone prepared to lead you to new opportunities. You gain greater faith in God because you see its effect on Paul day after day. You trust that God will guide, strengthen, and goad his workers to do more and more.

As I write, Paul's letter for the Roman followers of Christ has just arrived. Phoebe has personally shared his greetings to us. I was beaming with his report of how our work for the gospel had been shared in many congregations. Apparently, Andronicus and I had become "noteworthy among the apostles," that is, those who had seen the risen Lord and borne witness to him again and again. My hope is we will be reunited with Paul here in Rome. But we have not yet heard what has happened to Paul during his

IN THE WORDS OF JUNIA—PAUL'S FRIEND AND APOSTLE

visit to Jerusalem to take the collection from his churches to James and the believers there. May the Lord keep him safe, as there are those in that city that view him as a traitor to Judaism and would do him harm.

IN THE WORDS OF NERO—
PAUL'S EXECUTIONER

Emperor Nero Claudius Caesar Augustus Germanicus was born in AD 37 and probably committed suicide at the age of thirty in AD 68, after being declared a public enemy by the Roman Senate. As the fifth Roman emperor of the Julio-Claudian dynasty, he began his reign in AD 54, after his adoptive father Emperor Claudius was murdered.

Nero was far more popular with the common folk than with the socially elite and those in power. Suetonius claims that most Romans believed the Great Fire of Rome in AD 64 was started by Nero to clear land for his own use. Tacitus claims that Nero arrested Christians and blamed them for the fire. Suetonius and Sulpicius Severus claimed Nero tortured and killed Christians but for different reasons. Tertullian and Lactantius labeled Nero the first persecutor of Christians. Eusebius of Caesarea (c. 275–339) states that Paul was beheaded and Peter crucified during the reign of Nero.

Head of Nero now in the Glyptothek Museum, Munich, Germany

IN THE WORDS OF NERO—PAUL'S EXECUTIONER

Two sides of a gold coin made in AD 54 showing Nero and his mother Agrippina whom he killed in AD 59.

Nero coins which depict him rather accurately as an overweight ruler.

I can't believe that this trickster, this false Roman citizen, has slipped through my hands once already. When he was first brought to Rome for Roman justice, I was preoccupied with other things. Since the Sanhedrin didn't see fit to come and prosecute their case, I dismissed it precisely because Roman law gives the benefit of the doubt to Romans. And besides, I was not all that interested in governing at that point. Seneca and Burrus, my advisors, handled that while I pursued my real passion—the arts.

I've been emperor since AD 54. Now, ten years later there's been a Great Fire in Rome that burned for six days, died down, and burned three days more! Ten of my fourteen districts are badly damaged. Some Romans are whispering that I personally set it. I wasn't even in town when the first fire started. But I know they will at least say I ordered it. I have need of a scapegoat and I can think of none better or more despised than those *christianoi*—those partisans of Christ, as they are called. They are infecting even good elite Romans with their nonsense about some Jew they called the Christ. He is their Savior and Lord, not me the emperor! I really should do something about this insulting movement.

So, I have nothing to lose by fixing the blame on these partisans of Christ for the Great Fire. Most say it began in the merchant's shops near the Circus Maximus. I can bend the facts. There's also a pagan temple nearby and who would be more likely to set ablaze a pagan temple than those who don't believe in any gods except their One! And it won't be enough to make an example of a few minor followers of the Christ here in Rome. We need to cut off the head of the snake. I'm told this snake has two heads—Paul and Peter. We are going after both of them. Perhaps that will put an end to this "superstition," this false religion, and at the same time shift the blame from me to them for the Great Fire. That, in any case, is my plan.

I have sent members of the Praetorian Guard to track those men down. I hear that Paul is in Macedonia and Peter farther east. Never mind, we have the best military in the world. But we must track them down soon, as the opposition to me in Rome and the blame game has gotten intense. I will put out that fire by lighting another. I'm considering using Christians as human torches in the *Circus Maximus*. The mob in Rome loves such gory displays!

Oh, where is Seneca when I need his advice? Why has he not responded to my summons? I'm sure my men will soon find him. I am not a patient man, so the answer better come soon.[1]

---

1. After the first five years of Nero's reign, he paid less and less mind to Seneca's advice and became more and more isolated and arrogant. After the fire in Rome and Nero's attempt to fix blame on others, when Seneca had reason to believe that Nero himself had the fire set, Seneca took his life in AD 65, and so escaped the clutches of a narcissistic, ruthless ruler.

IN THE WORDS OF LUKE—
PAUL'S PHYSICIAN AND SCRIBE

Luke was a Greek God-fearer who was trained as a physician. As the widely accepted author of the Gospel of Luke and the book of Acts, he writes primarily to a Gentile audience, in particular, his noble friend Theophilus.

In Acts 28:16 Luke says, "When we came to Rome, Paul was allowed to live by himself, with the soldier who was guarding him." While under house arrest, Paul wrote (probably with a scribe's help) letters to Philemon, the Colossians, the Ephesians, and the Philippians. We first hear about Luke in Philemon 1:23–24: "Epaphras, my fellow prisoner in Christ Jesus, sends you greetings. And so do Mark, Aristarchus, Demas, and Luke, my fellow workers." In Colossians 4:14 we read, "Our dear friend Luke, the doctor, and Demas send greetings." At the end of his life in Rome, Paul writes 2 Timothy and notes that "only Luke is with me," apparently right to the end of Paul's life.

It's no surprise that Paul would travel and live under house arrest with a physician. He talks about his physical problems, his "thorn in the flesh" (2 Cor 12:7–9), which may have stemmed from his Damascus Road experience. Many believe Paul never regained his full sight. This would explain why he needs a scribe and sometimes mentions at the end of a document that he is adding a note in large script in his own hand (1 Cor 16:21; 2 Thess 3:17; Gal 6:11). Apparently, the Galatians would

St. Luke from an illuminated manuscript, c. AD 800.

have plucked out their own eyes to help him (Gal 4:15). Somewhat humorously, Paul referred to the high priest as a "white-washed" wall (Acts 23.3–5) because he apparently didn't recognize the high priest!

Luke would have been a real asset to Paul as his physician and as a learned scribe. He certainly wrote as a true historian in both his Gospel and his book of the Acts of the early church.

James Tissot (1836–1902), St. Luke, c. 1890. Brooklyn Museum.

I am a Greek and a physician by trade. I was itinerant, traveling regularly back and forth across the Aegean between the port city of Alexandria Troas and Philippi, my home in Macedonia. Yes, I am the true yokefellow, or companion, Paul once referred to in his Letter to the Philippians.[2] And

---

2. Phil 4:3. Gordon Fee put forth the idea that Luke was asked to stay behind and help the Christians in Philippi, his home area. See his *Philippians* (1995).

IN THE WORDS OF LUKE—PAUL'S PHYSICIAN AND SCRIBE

there was good reason for calling me his constant companion during the whole of his last major missionary tour. He needed my medical attention rather regularly.

Paul had a chronic eye problem going all the way back to his Damascus Road experience. Yes, he recovered some sight but his eyes were damaged by the brilliant light. This condition got progressively worse as he aged. The end result of his being beaten with rods, whipped repeatedly, and even stoned more than once, is that he suffered broken bones, deep bruises, and sores that required my ointments. When he lay down at night he was often in pain. All the walking as well resulted in dry skin and cracked feet—yet still he would not stop.

Then, of course, there were shipwrecks and the snake bite! He was a walking advertisement for why we need physicians. And there was some paradox about this because although some of his injuries healed well, his eye trouble did not. People are usually suspicious of a man who claims his Master was a healer and yet Paul himself was not healed, or worse claims he is a seer, and yet he has trouble seeing!

I was there on the occasion in Troas when "Lucky" fell out of the window. We raced to the ground floor to see if he survived. What I saw took my breath away. Eutychus was about to be taken away as a corpse but Paul laid hands on him and he quickened. His life breath returned into his body. I had only heard tales about resurrection but now I had the visual proof. And it frightened me. It led to questions like, what would Hippocrates have said about miracles? Why would one need a doctor if a miracle worker could heal better? I didn't have good answers to these questions.

It was on the third missionary journey that I realized we all needed a chronicle of the Way from its inception to the present. But at the time, I had not been to Jerusalem or Judaea. I didn't really know the story of the ministry of the Jesus before his death. I finally obtained a copy of Mark's Gospel, the earliest one. But I needed many more sources. It was not until well after Paul was martyred that I was able to compose my two-volume chronicle of salvation history for my patron Theophilus, in Macedonia. After traveling all those years with Paul, I settled down in Philippi, which gave me time for writing. By then, there had been a variety of other attempts to tell the story of the remarkable things that have happened among the followers of Jesus known as the Christ or the true Messiah.

You may rightly ask, how did I come to be part of Paul's traveling entourage? At first, I was just traveling from Troas back to Philippi along with Paul, and initially I just stayed in Philippi. But when Paul came back through Philippi later, he asked me to join him, told me he needed my services as a doctor, and so I became his attending physician, and also the doctor of various Christ followers we visited and stayed with. While the practice was not lucrative in the ordinary sense, it was rich in other ways. I got to be a part of a religious history I never knew was even important before I met Paul in Troas.

Once Paul and I delivered the collection from largely non-Jewish churches, and he had been placed under house arrest in Caesarea Maritima, I had two years to research and write about the movement. No one associated me with the prisoner. I was free to come and go, and to consult eyewitnesses and original preachers of the Word. I even got to speak with Miryam, Jesus' mother, and James, Jesus' brother, and Peter, the leader of the twelve apostles. They filled in the gaps. I also had time to do a great deal of reading in the Greek translation of the Hebrew Scriptures. I made myself a copy of key portions from the Law and the Prophets.

When we were finally sent packing from Caesarea Maritima to Rome, at the end of the sixth decade of the century, we had such an amazing adventure. I was reminded of the *Odyssey* and wrote up the account using language and imagery reminiscent of that great work. It was nice to use my Greek heritage in writing the end of the second chronicle. When we got to Rome, Paul was placed under house arrest. I stayed with him at first but then returned to Philippi and my practice there.

However, after two years Paul was released from house arrest. He headed back east to deal with problems and I joined him once more. In the end, he needed my help to compose letters to Titus and Timothy, whom he left in charge on Crete and in the city of Ephesus respectively. He could no longer see well enough to write letters that would be readable. It was in Macedonia that Nero's emissaries caught up with him again. They carted him and me back to Rome for another trial. This one would not go well. Nero was looking for a scapegoat to blame for the Great Fire, which rumor says he or his henchmen set.

The second letter to Timothy was heartbreaking to write. Paul was now in the Mamertine Prison waiting to be taken away for beheading. I alone could be with him as his physician.[3]

---

3. The Tullianum, later called Mamertinus, was a hellhole right on the northeastern slope of the Capitoline Hill that had been there for many centuries before the time of Paul. It faced the Forum and the Curia where the Senate met. It was so deep that no one could crawl out of it without a ladder. Probably both Paul and Peter ended up here.

IN THE WORDS OF LUKE—PAUL'S PHYSICIAN AND SCRIBE

Paul was brave to the very end. Unlike so many I have ministered to, Paul did not fear death, perhaps because he knew death would come swiftly since he would be beheaded. It was not long before Peter was also apprehended and martyred as well. At that point, when Christ followers were hiding out in various places including the catacombs, I managed a few interviews with Priscilla and Aquila and others in Rome. Then I decided to return home to Macedonia to write my Greek historical monograph similar to those I read during my education, such as the works of Xenophon, Thucydides, and Polybius.

We Greeks do not believe in simply writing up one's *own* memoirs, unlike the Romans such as Julius Caesar. History writing in the Greek mode required travel, interviews, inquiry, finding eyewitnesses or those who had contact with them. Fortunately for me, the trail had not gone cold. I interviewed many people, and I had my own eyewitness experiences to relate towards the end of the second volume. No one else is attempting such a chronicle, so I am thankful after all these years of travel and taking notes that my work will not go for naught.

I do indeed believe that those who forget the past are doomed to repeat it in the negative sense. But those who learn of the unique Christ and salvation history, and accept it, are bound for eternity. That is my belief and fervent prayer. May God use my words to his glory and to the edification of all who encounter them.

The Mamertine Prison in Rome, with an altar commemorating the imprisonment of Saints Peter and Paul there.

IN THE WORDS OF SIMON PETER—PAUL'S COUNTERPART IN MISSIONS

Simon Peter, along with his brother Andrew, was a fisherman living in Bethsaida. It was Andrew who first heard John the Baptizer preach about Jesus, and it was Andrew who first brought Simon to meet Jesus. Later, in Caesarea Philippi, when Peter boldly proclaims Jesus to be the Messiah, Jesus gave him the name Cephas, from the Aramaic and meaning rock or stone. Petros/Petra is the Greek and Latin versions from which we get the name Peter. He lived in Bethsaida along the northern coast of the Sea of Galilee. Peter was married (see 1 Cor 9:5). Nearby Capernaum was the home of his mother-in-law and the Synoptics all relate that she was healed by Jesus. But he left his family behind when he began traveling with Jesus (Mark 10:28).

Peter and Andrew were the first two apostles called by Jesus and eventually Peter became the leader of the Twelve. Jesus' death and resurrection proved to be difficult times for Peter—he denied Jesus three times, fled the scene, and later refused to believe the women who told him Jesus had risen. All was eventually forgiven by Jesus and Peter was restored as lead apostle.

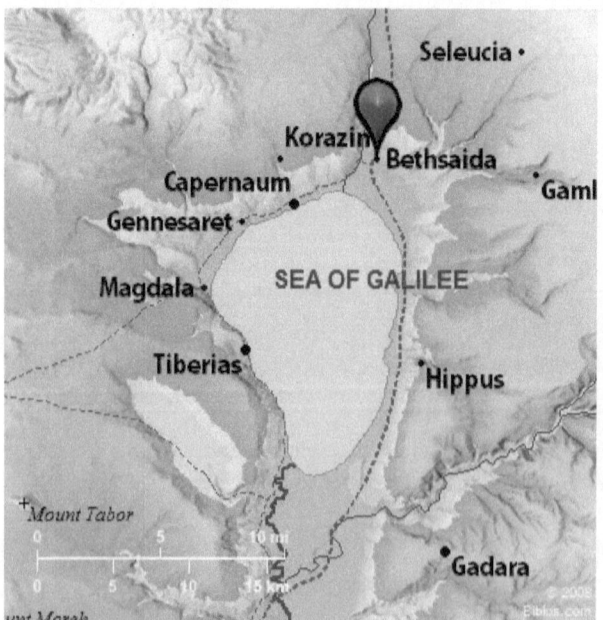

https://bibleatlas.org/full/bethsaida.htm.

After Pentecost, Peter spent

IN THE WORDS OF SIMON PETER

less time leading the church in Jerusalem and more time as a missionary. Jesus' brother, James the Just, became the leader of the Jerusalem church. Tradition holds that Peter eventually became Bishop of Rome and was crucified there—upside down.

Two representations of Simon Peter

Bartolomé Esteban Murillo (1617–1682),
St. Peter in Tears,
c. 1650.
Bilbao Fine Arts Museum, Bilbao, Spain.

Portrayed in tears over his denial of Jesus.

Peter Paul Rubens (1577–1640),
The Apostle St. Peter,
c. 1610–1612.
Museo Nacional del Prado, Madrid, Spain.

Portrayed in Peter's later years in papal regalia.

ENCOUNTERS WITH PAUL

Let's be clear about one thing from the start. Neither I nor Paul were founders of the Christ movement in Rome. It existed here long before either of us got there in the seventh decade of the first century. We helped the preexisting household groups with some guidance and oversight late in the game, after they had existed for more than two decades. Let's also be clear that Paul and I were not rivals. Yes, we had a heated exchange once in Antioch and, frankly, Paul was right to call me out for backing away from fellowship meals with Gentiles under pressure from Pharisaic Jewish followers of Christ visiting from Jerusalem.

We both accepted the division of labor laid out in Jerusalem early on. I was to concentrate on sharing the good news with Jews and Paul to focus on Gentiles. We both agreed the good news about Christ was for the Jew first! Naturally we both started with synagogues and other Jewish settings. Furthermore, ours was not a territorial matter, with Paul going to one region and me to another, although both of us were trying to start assemblies where none existed. This got complicated when both of us were in Corinth at different times! We even shared co-workers occasionally. This was perfectly natural since we were working towards the same end—sharing the good news of salvation in Christ with the world in which we lived.

Sometimes I am asked what happened to my family, including my wife, when I started traveling outside Galilee and Judaea. During Jesus' ministry, I left them all at home in Capernaum by the Sea of Galilee and even spoke of this with Jesus. However, nearly ten years after the death of Jesus, I did take my wife with me on mission tours, leaving our adult children to continue our fishing business on the Sea of Galilee.[1] Paul, however, lost his immediate family when he devoted himself to Christ. Only his sister and her son would even talk to him or help him when he was in Jerusalem.[2] His co-workers became a kind of family to him, giving the terms "brothers and sisters in Christ" a more concrete meaning, as we are all part of the family of faith.

I must tell you that Paul was indeed a hard act to follow. So many places I went, Paul had been there before me and even some Jews had been converted. For this and other reasons I concentrated on areas where he spent little or no time. I focused on Jews who were literally resident aliens in those areas, Jews who had become thoroughly Hellenized even to the

---

1. In 1 Corinthians 9:5 Paul says, "Don't we have the right to take a believing wife along with us, as do the other apostles and the Lord's brothers and Cephas?"

2. See Acts 23, where his sister's son reported the plot to kill Paul to the centurion.

point of becoming pagan in some ways. There is a long history of Jews being deported to regions in Asia, like Galatia and Cappadocia, as craftsmen, mine workers, and slaves. It is a vast territory, and we traveled more than we stayed in one place.

Some of these Jews had even become idolaters, sad to say. But Christ gave them an opportunity to reappropriate some of their Jewish dreams and heritage. What I had to emphasize to them, given the suffering and abuse they had undergone as a despised minority, was that Christ himself was not exempt from suffering and abuse! I put it this way with the help of Silvanus, who wrote a letter for me:[3]

> For it is commendable if someone bears up under the pain of unjust suffering because they are conscious of God. But how is it to your credit if you receive a beating for doing wrong and endure it? But if you suffer for doing good and you endure it, this is commendable before God. To this you were called, because Christ suffered for you, leaving you an example, that you should follow in his steps. [Isaiah 53:9 says], "He committed no sin, and no deceit was found in his mouth." When they hurled their insults at him, he did not retaliate; when he suffered, he made no threats. Instead, he entrusted himself to him who judges justly. [Remember Isaiah 53:4–6]: "He himself bore our sins" in his body on the cross, so that we might die to sins and live for righteousness; "by his wounds you have been healed." For "you were like sheep going astray," but now you have returned to the Shepherd and Overseer of your lives.[4]

Of course, I knew I was not exempt from such suffering. Indeed, Christ had told me the day was coming when I would be bound and led off to execution.[5] Fortunately, that day has not come yet. Now that I am finally in Rome there is much to be done! The Jewish and Gentile followers here are not united and are rarely if ever meeting together. It is hard to overcome some of the anti-Semitism that is even latent in some of the Gentile converts who are young in the faith. The thing about being part of a new religious movement is that the ground is constantly shifting under your feet, by which I mean things are constantly changing.

Converts are mobile, coming and going from Rome, but overall, the number of converts keeps increasing and we must find new places and ways to integrate them into household communities. This is especially hard

---

3. I.e., 1 Peter.
4. 1 Pet 2:19–25.
5. John 21:18–19.

when we are dealing with those young in the faith. They need discipling! They need an older follower to help them grow in the faith. Priscilla and Aquila and Andronicus and Junia can only do so much.

I sense my time is short. I am thankful Silas and I got that letter done before the end. I am also hoping Apollos and Timothy are on their way. I am sure God is with us and nothing is going to snuff out the light of Christ, which continues to spread across our world. So here is my charge to those who lead each of these household assemblies: "To the elders among you, I appeal as a fellow elder and a witness of Christ's sufferings who also will share in the glory to be revealed: Be shepherds of God's flock that is under your care, watching over them—not because you must, but because you are willing, as God wants you to be; not pursuing dishonest gain, but eager to serve; not lording it over those entrusted to you, but being examples to the flock. And when the Chief Shepherd appears, you will receive the crown of glory that will never fade away."[6]

---

6. 1 Pet 5:1–4.

IN THE WORDS OF CLEMENT—
PAUL'S SUCCESSOR IN ROME

Clement of Rome was born in AD 35 and died in AD 99. Tradition says he died in Greece under the reign of Emperor Trajan. Clement was possibly consecrated bishop or overseer in Rome by Peter, before Peter died in the late 60s. He is also honored as among the first apostolic fathers of the church, along with Polycarp and Ignatius of Antioch. Probably the oldest church document in existence outside the New Testament is his letter to the church in Corinth, which indicates that he carefully read Paul's first letter to the Corinthians.

Clement of Rome,
11th century mosaic,
St. Sophia Church.
Kyiv, Ukraine.

ENCOUNTERS WITH PAUL

I was a co-worker of Paul towards the latter phase of his ministry in the eastern part of the empire.[1] Later in the century, I was in Rome and became an *episkopos*[2] after the apostles Paul and Peter were martyred. Paul had a big impact on me in so many ways. I was honored to work side by side with him in the proclamation of the good news.

One of my responsibilities was to write and give direction to various of the Pauline congregations after Paul died, especially those in Corinth. So, I wrote them a letter based on Paul's own famous letter he wrote them some thirty years earlier. The same problems of factions and disputes were still plaguing them. I will share with you two excerpts from my lengthy letter, which is really more of a rhetorical discourse than a letter.

> Because of the sudden and numerous misfortunes and setbacks we have experienced [here in Rome] we realize we have been slow to turn our attention to the things causing disputes among you. They involve that vile and profane "stasis"/faction that is alien and foreign to the elect of God, a "stasis"/faction stirred up by a few headstrong persons to such a degree of madness that your renowned reputation worthy of everyone's love has been slandered.
>
> And all of you used to be humble minded, not arrogant, being submissive [to the elders] rather than forcing submission, giving more gladly than receiving, being satisfied by the things provided by Christ. You heeded his words, storing them up in your innermost parts, and his suffering was before your eyes. Thus, a deep and rich peace was given to all and an unquenchable desire for good deeds, and a full outpouring of the Holy Spirit was upon everyone. You were sincere and blameless and bore no evil thoughts towards one another. You despised every faction and division. You were clothed with a highly virtuous and honorable manner of life and in all reverence of God you accomplished all things, and the righteous demands of the Lord were written on your hearts.[3]

This, of course, was my attempt to establish rapport with my audience, to make them favorably disposed to hear the rest of my discourse. The truth is that the Corinthians were just as spiritually gifted and just as divided near

---

1. Phil 4:3.

2. An overseer. The term later meant bishop, a specific kind of overseer.

3. These are excerpts from the first two chapters of 1 Clement. I am following the Loeb translation by B. Ehrman (*The Apostolic Fathers* [2003]), making a few changes where I thought it was warranted.

IN THE WORDS OF CLEMENT—PAUL'S SUCCESSOR IN ROME

the end of the century as they had been in Paul's time. I even tried to appeal to the martyrdoms of our leaders to get them to behave.

I said to them:

> We should consider the examples of our own generation. Because of jealousy and envy the greatest and most upright pillars were persecuted, and they struggled in the contest even unto death. We should set before our eyes the good apostles like Peter who, because of unrighteous zeal, bore many hardships not just once or twice but many times. Having borne his witness he went to his deserved place of glory. Because of zeal and strife Paul pointed the way to the prize for endurance. Seven times he bore chains; he was sent into exile and stoned. He served as a herald/preacher in both the East and the West and he received a noble reputation for his faith by teaching righteousness to the whole world. And he came to the limits of the West bearing his witness before rulers. Thus, he was liberated from this world and taken up to the holy place, having become the greatest example of perseverance.[4]

The attentive reader of my discourse will have recognized that I was following along not only with Paul's famous Letter to the Corinthians but also the Greek Old Testament plus Apollos's Letter to the Hebrews. Basically, I decided to put everything into a single discourse, divided into sections, so it could be used on a series of occasions of household congregational meetings. The problem was not just divisions but failure to heed their own elders and overseers. If even Paul had trouble sorting such things out in his day, I thought that a more detailed discourse dealing with the full scope of the reported problems was the only way forward. I tried to shame them into better behavior by talking about the martyrdoms we endured during the reign of Nero and, more recently, under Domitian.

I am an old man now. My eyes have grown dim, but my mind is clear in regard to the example Paul set for us all to follow. No one, other than Christ himself, has done more to establish our faith! In essence, this means following a new covenant that preaches right-standing with God by grace through faith in our Lord and Savior Christ. It involves Jew and Gentile united in Christ himself who has broken down the barriers between the two groups. I thank God regularly for Paul and his work. He had a great

---

4. This is an excerpt from 1 Clement 5, and again I have followed Ehrman but with some emendations. The reference to the limits of the West has been much debated but the immediate context favors the conclusion that Clement is referring to Rome itself, rather than Spain.

impact not only on my life but on so many lives. I pray that that impact will continue until our Lord returns in glory to fully establish his reign on earth as it is in heaven.

EPILOGUE

MY TWO BOOKS, *ENCOUNTERS with Jesus* and *Encounters with Paul*, focus on historical people who had first-century encounters with Jesus and Paul, both positive and negative. Admittedly, however, Paul is not of the same ilk as Jesus. Jesus is a living Lord, the divine Son of God the Father, whom Christians and others still encounter in prayer and worship whenever two or more are gathered in his Name. Paul, for all of his impact even today, is simply another human being like us, an ancient historical figure who encountered the living Lord and became Jesus' advocate and emissary.

Nevertheless, people today do encounter Paul in his vivid and lively letters, the accounts of his life in Acts, and through second-century and later documents. These range from the document known as *Paul and Thecla* (see the picture on the frontispiece of this book) to the wonderful homilies by John Chrysostom about Paul, his life, and teaching.[1]

For all Christians, the impact of Paul in his letters has been enormous. Anyone who has studied the lives of the church leaders before and after the Reformation will know this. Luther himself famously said, in his usual hyperbolic manner, that he had wed himself to Galatians! Paul became the paradigm for preaching and teaching. The call of Paul to "be imitators of me as I am of Christ" was taken very seriously.

But it's not only the local church leaders who have been shaped by Paul, it's also the missionaries. Think of all the missionaries who, like Paul, traversed the world sharing the gospel. Or think of the evangelists like Billy Graham, who were instruments of God sparking revival in many countries. And this sort of impact is still happening today for good and for God.

Now admittedly, there are some issues with focusing so much on Paul that we neglect Jesus and his teachings. Seeing Jesus through the lens of Paul is not adequate, especially when we may encounter Jesus himself more directly as the living Lord. Nevertheless, it is my hope that these two little books will encourage us all to not only appreciate but seek to encounter

---

1. See M. Mitchell's splendid book, *The Heavenly Trumpet* (2002).

both Jesus and Paul more intimately. The outcome, I would hope, can only result in a more healthy and less biblically illiterate church.

www.ingramcontent.com/pod-product-compliance
Lightning Source LLC
Chambersburg PA
CBHW030901170426
43193CB00009BA/707